Joy's Journey

Joy's Journey

JOY ELLIOTT

Library of Congress Control Number:		2021923068
ISBN:	Hardcover	978-1-6641-9407-6
	Softcover	978-1-6641-9406-9
	eBook	978-1-6641-9405-2

Print information available on the last page.

Rev. date: 12/28/2021

To order additional copies of this book, contact:
Xlibris
844-714-8691
www.Xlibris.com
Orders@Xlibris.com
833340

CHAPTER 1

January 7, 2017

The pungent smell of disinfectant pierced the air, and the dreary white of the hospital seemed to surround us in a cocoon of uncertainty and fear. Amidst all the quiet chaos, my husband gripped my hand with all the strength he seemed to have left in his body.

"When I wake up, we will go home," he whispered. "Okay?" The words struggled to leave his mouth, but his unwavering optimism and the need to comfort me warmed my heart, the same way it had done so many times before.

"Yes, sweetheart, when you wake up, we will go home," I replied.

But I knew, despite his steadfast optimism, that I would be going home by myself that day.

And thus, with no pomp and ceremony, ended thirty-five years with the love of my life. Thirty-five years of travel, learning, love, and wonder. Thirty-five years of more than I ever expected or could ever explain. The light of my life was gone, and I was utterly clueless as to what the rest of my life had in store for me.

All I was left with was pain, loss, and more loneliness than I knew to bear.

My husband's illness had completely ravaged him as a person for a while, and for the past eighteen months, we both knew that the unspeakable was going to happen. I thought this very knowledge would give me strength and a sense of readiness and preparation.

However, I found out soon enough that not even the most detailed itinerary of my husband's future well-being could have prepared me for the moment he was taken from me.

First, there was the undeniable physical pain, so all-consuming and intense that it felt like a boiling sore covering most of my body. I then knew the true meaning of heartbreak—there was a constant, aching pain in my chest that refused to leave. The shock and grief of losing him manifested itself quite physically throughout me, and the pain was growing and whirling and screaming. It was complete and utter anguish.

Simple tasks, like sitting up straight or falling asleep, became monstrous hurdles that I did not know how to face. Being alone with my thoughts became impossibility, as more than a few minutes of ruminating over my loss left me paralyzed, unable to think or move. Thus, the only way I could hold myself together was to keep frantically busy. I cleaned the house day and night, scrubbing all the tiles with a small brush. I even scoured the inside of the fireplace, attacking corners, nooks, and crannies I had never thought of cleaning before.

The thought of meeting other people immediately after seemed like an arduous task I simply did not have the strength for. However, after a few weeks, I called a dear friend and arranged to meet her for breakfast. I thought I was ready; I prepared for socializing, smiling, and talking.

As I sat at a table alone waiting for her to arrive, I nervously stirred my coffee and rehearsed a speech about how I was okay. Yes, of course, it was painful, but I had it under control. But when she walked through the door, I was filled with crushing anguish once again. How could I possibly pretend I was fine when I was not? Despite my best efforts, I burst into tears before her eyes even located me.

For as long as I could remember, I have fantasized about finding a sleepy village somewhere in the old world, untouched by society's current advancements and fast-paced nature. There, I would make a cozy spot for myself and stay, settling into a routine, until I befriended all the locals and thoroughly absorbed their culture. Then, I would move on and do it all over again. However, my fantasy remained just that—a whimsical dream I never got to bring to fruition. Life, with all of its scheduling, plans, and routines, happened, and I was never in a position to pull off my plan. And now, of course, I was too old to have time for this particular daydream.

But after the loss of my husband and amid my grief, panic, and loneliness, I let my mind run free and began to formulate another plan.

I decided to go see Europe. Yes, all of Europe—especially the less advertised spots, the historic areas of eastern Europe from Macedonia to Estonia. When I put my idea forward to those closest to me, I was told that I was too old (eighty-three) for such an idea.

My response was practiced and uncomplicated: Yes, I was fully aware of my age and its implications, but here was the thing, next year I will be older, so I don't dare postpone. How horrible to wait and never get to realize this dream of mine.

I had traveled quite a lot with my husband, but I always regretted having to come home before I began to get acquainted with the culture, people, and particular quirks of a specific place. Usually, we would be packing up and leaving in about two weeks, the standard length of a vacation in the US.

I had heard about an EU rail pass, which allowed you to travel for twenty-one days in two months at a considerable discount. I knew I wanted more than just two months to fulfill my desire to explore and understand the areas I wanted to visit, so I bought two passes. I purchased a round-trip ticket to London, going in May and returning in October. My plan was to stay in London as long as I wanted and then travel all over Europe by rail and return to London to fly home in October. I had been to London before, but my trips were always cut short sooner than I wanted. This time, I made a firm resolution that I would stay until I was satiated with London.

Of course, in the past, when I traveled, I was never alone. I was about to find out how traveling alone was different. I do not mean alone in a group tour; I mean well and truly alone. The thought filled me with both nervous anticipation and excitement.

I have always been a shy person, and so was my husband.

However, we were both successful career people, so our shyness was not a setback there. We could talk to people when we had a reason to do so, but we did not approach strangers to strike up a conversation or in an attempt to make friends.

We had a modest social life. What mattered most to us was that we had each other and that was enough.

I believe I was a lot shier than most people, but I didn't consider it a problem yet. However, I learned that if you decide to be a solo traveler, severe shyness is a debilitating problem, and moderate shyness is a terrible inconvenience. My shyness manifested itself through all my interactions during my strange and fantastic trip, but I managed to overcome it because I simply had to. Overcoming my shyness and anxiety led me down many paths of adventure and fun and into enticing places and conversations I could never have imagined experiencing!

I learned about solo travelers staying in hostels. What better way to let the culture and atmosphere of a place sink in to your wanderlust than staying at a hostel? They offered a good opportunity to mingle with other travelers and were affordable too. Also hostels are the most economically feasible way for a single person to travel. In hotels you always pay for two, even when you are alone.

I booked two weeks in London and decided to plan the rest of the trip spontaneously. I wanted to remain preoccupied enough during my trip to not let my recent grief overcome me. I knew I could not accomplish my intention by traveling in luxury. I must make the trip as challenging as possible.

And so begins the story of how I made a dream come true—a love note to all the cities I visited, people I met, and experiences I had.

May 2017

My journey began when I arrived in London. From previous experiences, I knew to go downstairs at Heathrow Airport to the underground station, buy a public transit pass, pick up a map, and get downtown economically. I had already researched the hostel address, so I knew which underground line to use and when to change. Almost immediately, I had to face the first challenge of my trip.

I had two cases, one carry-on and one larger. The London underground is *very* underground, and only a few stations have elevators (called lifts in the UK). Mostly, they have lots of stairs, which was definitely a setback for me and my heavy bags. Already, my journey was proving to be very difficult.

When I arrived at the station nearest to my reserved hostel, I got off the subway, hailed a cab, gave the driver my hostel address, and piled in.

The driver found the street, even the address, but we could not find the hostel. He drove back and forth until finally, he decided it must be where he last looked, so he went knocking on doors. Sure enough, the hostel was above an off track betting office, but there was no sign showing the hostel's existence. Most frustrating of all was that there were even more stairs to climb!

This hostel did not measure up to the favorable experiences I have had with hostels in the past. It seemed almost like a menagerie, with big dogs underfoot in the kitchen and pet birds flying in the common room. US health inspectors would have shut it down immediately. London inspectors will probably shut it down, too, when they find it! To add insult to injury, it was run by an American woman who was unlike anyone I had ever known in America.

The shower stalls were so small you couldn't lift your elbows and you had to put in a new coin for every 5 minutes. *Oh, well*, I thought to myself, *I would put this stressful experience behind and enjoy London.*

I quickly realized that I had been in London enough times before to not be a tourist anymore. I had seen all the sights and done all the activities. Now, I had no desire to repeat my previous endeavors again, especially alone.

So I used my pass on the city transport and rode the city buses to the farthest suburbs to look at the neighborhoods. I got off at will and walked a lot. On one of my outings, I discovered a spot near Paddington Station called Little Venice. It had canals, houseboats, lots of flowers, and a water taxi. I rode the water taxi and saw the backyards of the most elegant homes and palaces in London. It also went through the zoo and finished up at a delightfully quaint neighborhood market.

One day, while walking into a cold wind with my brolly, I was pelted with nickel-sized chunks of ice. Hail! I hadn't expected that and wasn't dressed for it. I did not even have spare room in my bags for winter clothes. However, the hail was increasing in speed and ferocity, and the wind felt like it was nipping at my hands and face. I needed a solution, and fast. Thankfully, I spotted a thrift store and got myself decked out in temporary winter gear.

I also learned something unique about hostels that I hadn't thought of before. Previously, since my husband and I traveled as a couple, we would book a private room. This time, I booked the female dorm. That means you have no privacy, and you have to talk to strangers. Does this idea make you feel uneasy? It certainly stirred me, but only at the beginning. To my surprise, I gradually learned that the very best thing about hostels is the people you meet. Hotels are polite, clean, and have lots of services, but they get lonely. Hostels, on the other hand, are community affairs. The travelers there were young, mostly college students, and I was apprehensive about how I would be accepted, but I needn't have been concerned. Youngsters who travel are the cream of the crop! They all seemed genuinely delighted that I had joined them.

My bed was in an all-female dorm, and with the girls milling about constantly, I did not get a chance to feel lonely. I had no time to think about or nurse my grief.

One girl had left her job as a primary school teacher in Australia to come to London alone. She was looking for a job as a nanny and moved out after finding one within a week. Another girl was from Paris and was traveling with four brothers. I chatted with all of them in the common room. They were here for just a few days and were having so much fun. Then, they dropped a mini bomb on me! They were Muslims! I told them I didn't know any Muslims, and I thought I was afraid of them. They were genuinely amused by the encounter and taught me a lot about themselves and their ways of life. Another girl, who was from Eastern Europe, spoke little English. She was looking for a job too, any job! I felt sorry for her because of the language barrier.

I met an amiable young man over breakfast. We went to the National Gallery together and then had lunch. He was Russian, and the only Russian individual I have ever known. His name was Jacob, which he spelled Y-A-K-O-V. We exchanged Facebook friendship. I was curious about how Jacob could afford to travel so much. I established, through nosy interrogation, that his family was not wealthy, but he had worked a regular job, saved his money, and then quit to go see the world. What intelligence and bravery for such a young man!

Over the coming months, I followed Jacob online as he toured the world and met the love of his life. I watched as they two hitchhiked through Iran, hiked the Camino de Santiago pilgrimage in Spain, spent a month in Myanmar, and then went to China to get married. They have since settled in Montenegro, but they still travel, and he earns money online as a life coach.

By the end of my second week, I decided that I had enough of London sooner than I expected. I had been hailed on twice, seen many things, and was now anxious to move on. I found the rail station and went in with the idea to get on with my travels and explore places I had not seen.

I should probably fill you in on a bit of background. My darling husband, John, was from Belfast, Northern Ireland. His family was still there. I had been close to his family, but I was apprehensive about visiting them this time. Would they still be as anxious for me to call now that I couldn't bring their loved one? Even thinking about that opened my sore of grief again. Was it somehow my fault that he was gone? Did I not take good enough care of him? I knew, to soothe my anxiety, I must visit his family and find out for sure.

I had told my extended family in Belfast that I would be there after my London visit, but now, I wanted to go early. They had recently moved house and were still getting settled. I didn't want to call and say I was coming *now*! But I also didn't want to stay in London. So I went to the rail station for a chat. I had not activated my EU rail pass yet as they are not valid in the UK. I decided to use those later.

Arriving at the counter, I smiled at the ticket agent. "How much for a rail ticket to Belfast?" I inquired.

"Sixty-four pounds," he replied.

"Do I need to book and buy in advance?" I questioned, hoping I could save some money through an earlier booking.

"No," he stated. "Same price now or when you travel."

I was still debating about what to do with the extra week. I was nervous about showing up at my relatives' a week early. Then it dawned on me! A rail ticket to Belfast included a ferry leg. To connect to the ferry, we had to go through Glasgow, Scotland. So I decided to spend a week in Glasgow.

I canceled the remaining week in my hostel, packed my bags, and arrived at the rail station early the next day.

"Must I complete the journey in one day, or can I layover a few days in Glasgow?" I asked the ticket agent.

"No, you must complete the journey in one day," was his disappointing reply.

"Well, then, how much for a ticket just to Glasgow?" I asked nervously.

"Sixty-four pounds."

"What?! That is the same as a ticket to Belfast, and Glasgow is a stop on the way to Belfast! How much for a ticket from Glasgow to Belfast?"

"Sixty-four pounds," he repeated once again.

"That doesn't make any sense at all!" I replied indignantly.

The agent just smiled and said, "I know."

My mind was a muddle. I couldn't think what to do, but I had to decide. It was nearly time for the train to go.

Resolutely, I made my decision. "Give me a ticket to Belfast."

On the train, though, I kept thinking. I could get off in Glasgow, no one would know, but then it would cost another sixty-four pounds to go on to Belfast. I hadn't booked a room, and I wasn't that excited about Glasgow anyway. John and I had been there and loved it, but I wanted to avoid the places we visited together because it was too painful.

So I stayed on the train and continued my journey to the ferry and Belfast.

I arrived in Belfast just past 9:00 p.m. My relatives were not expecting me for days. I had been there before, but I had never seen any hotels. On previous trips, I was cared for by John and his family, so I wasn't required to notice much of anything. Lodging in all the UK is quite different than what I was used to in the US. There were not hotels or motels at every corner. The hotels that did exist were first class, quite expensive, and previously booked. The British and Irish rely much more on bed-and-breakfasts and advance booking.

It was cold, dark, and rainy when I arrived. After disembarking the ferry, I looked about and saw something off into the distance that looked like a city bus. As I pulled my two suitcases over, I saw a man talking to the driver. I couldn't help overhearing their conversation, so I climbed aboard and said to the man, "Did I hear you ask the driver about a hotel?"

"Yes," he replied. "The driver said he thinks he remembers where there used to be one."

The bus went downtown to the end of the line. This was the last run, as buses did not run at night. I overheard the driver give the man directions to where he thought a hotel used to be. I didn't speak due to my shyness. So when the man started off down the street, I, with my two bags, went scurrying behind, hoping not to make it evident that I was following him.

He crossed the street and turned right. I turned right without crossing the road, but I could still see him. After a few blocks, he turned left. By now, I was a bit behind, but I finally glimpsed a sign of hope. I was sure I could see a sign that said Hotel.

The man was inside already, and I was getting close when he came dashing back out of the hotel, walked right up to me, and said, "They only have one room. I'm willing to share it if you are."

The very idea that he suggested was so far out of my comfort zone that I was rendered mute. I was raised by a very religious mother and was old and set in my ways. Being very morally conservative, I couldn't believe what I just heard! It sounded like a thunder clap. My thoughts were frenzied, and my mind screamed, *My God! I can't do this!* A more rational part of my brain was quick to respond: *What else am I going to do? This town is locked down. The buses have stopped, and you have no idea how to find another hotel. Also, it is cold and raining.*

Then, another rebuttal, *He might be lying!* But also, if he was not lying, then he was a nice man. He could have just taken the room and gone up before I got there.

Finally, I realized, *You can't stand here any longer with your mouth hanging open! You look like a fool!* Say something!

"It's okay with me as long as there are two beds," I replied, much to my own shock.

"Well, let's go ask them." He smiled.

Now, I had a new problem: keeping from blushing like a schoolgirl when talking to the hotel clerk.

"Yes, there are two beds," the clerk assured us.

I said I wanted the room for two nights. I paid with my card, while the man gave me cash for half of one night, and we went upstairs. He was in his seventies, I in my eighties, so what do you suppose we got up to?

We talked and giggled all night long. We told each other life stories and cracked each other up with quips and anecdotes. David, British, had a lifetime career of posing as a British professor in a British village tourist attraction in Paris. All he had to do was look and sound like a British professor, which he couldn't help doing anyway. I thought that was so funny. What a fantastic job! We got very little sleep. I hadn't had so much fun in ages.

The next day, we had breakfast, and David went on his way. I had errands to run, which filled my day. I felt grubby with all the nonstop traveling and knew I didn't want to face my relatives like that. I got a haircut and a manicure, but I could not find anyone to do a pedicure. Apparently, it didn't get hot enough in Northern

Ireland to require sandals. This was a stark contrast to my life back in Phoenix, where pedicures are an essential part of grooming. I bought a box of hair color and went back to the hotel room. Just as I finished up the process of dying my hair, there was a knock on the door; it was David.

"Can I stay another night?" he inquired.

"Of course!" I replied. I was glad to have his company for another day. "Come on in!"

We went out to dinner and then visited the Crown, the oldest pub in Belfast. It was beautiful.

We were tired, so we slept more than the previous night, but there was still plenty of talking and giggling.

The next day, David went on his way, this time for good, and I got up the nerve to call my relatives.

To my relief, I needn't have been worried. They were as loving and welcoming as ever. I had a wonderful week with them. We spent a lot of time discussing my plans for the summer, poring over my EU rail maps, and discussing all the faraway places I was planning to visit. I didn't tell them about David, as I wasn't quite ready to share that experience yet. I was afraid they would think their brother's widow had gone totally wild already. My sister-in-law taught me how to install and use WhatsApp so I could talk to her for free from anywhere in the world. I could even do video calls, the idea of which horrified me. But I may as well get used to it.

My relatives live in Bangor, which is a beautiful little seaside resort near Belfast. The only downside to my visit was that this was John's hometown, and we had spent a lot of time here together. When I walked on the streets, I couldn't help peering into every face to see if it was him. But he wasn't there. The disappointment and sadness settled on me with a horrible finality.

By this point in my travels, I became aware that I had over packed by a lot, so I downsized. I left a heavy carry-on with my relatives and promised to come back in October to pick it up. I went forward with a single, much lighter bag.

When I left Belfast, John's brother took me to the rail terminal. It seemed we were closer now since John was gone. It was because we both loved John so much, and when he was there, we centered our attention on him. But now, he was gone, and we were forced to see each other. And of course, John's brother's wife became the dearest friend I could ever hope to have.

My plan was to activate my rail pass, take a train to the southern tip of Ireland, and then a ferry to France. In a way, this was the beginning of my adventure because this was where I made the startling jump into a non-English-speaking country.

CHAPTER 2

When I left Belfast, my schedule entailed arriving at the ferry station in Rosslare three to four hours earlier than my connecting ferry.

I was settled on the train in Belfast when an announcement blared through the speakers stating that there was a problem on the track. A chorus of groans and sighs erupted throughout the carriage, and all the passengers began recollecting their recently stowed belongings. We were all herded back onto the platform and directed to a bus stop. The buses that came to collect us took us out of the way and then onto another train that finally brought us back to the original track but below the problem.

This inconvenience caused me to arrive at the ferry station barely in time for my connection.

While I hurriedly got onto my ferry, the agent informed me that there were no berths left and that they only had reclining chairs. I said that was fine—I had slept in reclining chairs before, and they were pretty comfortable. I could easily relax on one of those through the nineteen-hour ferry ride from Rosslare, Ireland, to Cherbourg, France.

Unfortunately, I never found the reclining chair I paid for. I didn't ask for help—that would have required approaching a stranger, and my shyness would not have allowed me to do such a thing. So I just slept on a bench in the bar. It wasn't all that bad, but it was certainly a high price to pay for maintaining my habitual shyness.

I arrived in Cherbourg, France, at about 6:00 p.m. the following day. I had a hostel reserved in Paris, but it was for tomorrow and it was a further four-hour train ride. I didn't want to arrive in Paris in the middle of the night, so I decided to stay the night in Cherbourg and continue my travels the following day.

However, there was one problem—I didn't have a room reserved in Cherbourg. It made sense to stay near the train station so I could wake up the following day and be promptly on my way.

I found a taxi at the ferry station and asked the driver to take me to the train station. I could have said I was looking for a hotel, and the driver might have helped, but that would have required too much talking, and asking for help was not something that I was yet comfortable with.

After a short drive in a gentle rain, we arrived at the train station. I exited the taxi and looked around, scanning for a place where I could stay, when my eyes finally fell upon a little hotel with a No Vacancy sign.

"Yes!" I said to myself, ever the optimist. "Surely they would have one bed for little ol' me."

I rang the bell, prepared to inquire if I could stay for just one night. A lady answered the bell, said *"No vacancy"* loudly and *slammed* the door. I didn't get to say a single word. That was my introduction to non-English speakers. They must get very frustrated with tourists, especially when they ignore signs.

The night was already dark and cold and drizzling rain. I walked to the corner, looked both ways, and decided to turn *that* way instead of *this.*

With Big Red (my suitcase) for company, I began walking beside a river aimlessly and endlessly.

Finally, I came across a line of shops, which were mostly closed, but one small flower shop was open.

I went in but would speak to no one until all the other customers had finished their shopping and gone since I knew they would stare at the English-speaking lady. Finally, when the last customer bundled up her purchases and left, I asked the clerk for directions to a hotel. She, too, spoke no English but did understand the word *hotel* and began talking, waving her arms, and pointing. I got the idea.

Keeping her directions in mind, I exited the shop and walked farther. After crossing a bridge and walking some more, I finally saw a hotel sign. Much to my disappointment, a closer inspection revealed another No Vacancy sign. After my first experience, I wasn't about to risk another door slammed in my face.

As I walked farther, I was faced with let-down upon let-down, coming across more hotels with No Vacancy signs.

Finally, after a lot more searching and walking, I came upon a hotel without a No Vacancy sign! I rushed in, thanking my lucky stars.

The lady at the counter told me that there was just one room left and quoted quite a high price.

Despite this, I found myself immediately exclaiming, "I'll take it!"

This hotel was small—it had no door attendant and no elevator. I wrestled my bag up a dark, narrow, and winding stairway. The hallway was unilluminated, so I began to feel around until I found a light switch. Warm yellow light flooded the hallway, allowing me to find my room. When I got in, I was pleasantly surprised to find a little piece of heaven! The room was clean and had a welcome warm and dry atmosphere. The setup looked rather cheery, and best of all, it was private and secure! I spread my wet clothes all out to dry, took a hot shower, and slept like a rock.

The following day, I felt great! I dressed warmly, wrangled my suitcase down the stairs, and looked about. The area seemed rather different in the sunlight, and as I was enjoying the view, my eyes fell upon something that made me laugh in disbelief. I couldn't believe what I saw! Just over there was the rail station. I had walked in a big circle. I should have turned *this* way instead of *that*. At that moment, I swore never again to enter a town without a room reservation.

I had my hostel's address in Paris, but I had no idea where it was or how to get there. I did have a smartphone, but I was completely unaware of its magic capabilities. I knew how to make hostel reservations, but that was all! I watched in awe as others got the answer to any question instantly. Google Maps was still wholly unimaginable to me and, therefore, unusable.

The train that took me to Paris left me three levels below ground. I dragged my bag up all those stairs, as European train stations have no elevators or escalators. "Get used to it!" I told myself. To be fair, they did have friendly people, and I got a lot of help all over Europe. Sometimes, if I was too beat to carry my heavy luggage, I would just stand around for a bit and try to look pitiful, and someone would usually rescue me. Incidentally, my rescuer was often a woman.

I found my way out to a large square but saw little in the form of hope: no information signs and no taxis. But I did see a large, fancy-looking hotel. Good! I am familiar with those. I knew hotels would have consiglieres and they would speak English.

I went and approached the consigliere's desk, bold as brass, trying to give the impression that I was a guest. I showed the address, and they told me how to find it, even going so far as to print a map for me. It involved the tube, which was back at the train station, four levels down. I followed the directions, which included a change and some walking time, but I found the hostel. This whole endeavor required effort and took lots of time, which was the entire point of my journey in the first place—I was challenging myself consistently.

Once again, I came across a lot of interesting individuals in the dorms that I stayed in. One of the women in my dorm was a sixty-five-year-old lady who had just come over from London for the weekend and brought her bike. I was impressed. I didn't feel so unique anymore.

The next day, I took the tube back downtown to sightsee and found a hop-on, hop-off bus. I had learned years ago how to use them economically—the trick is not to hop off!

If you hop off, then the lines at the attraction, plus the wait for the next bus, means that you get to experience little and do not get your money's worth from the bus. If you intend on using a hop-on, hop-off bus for sightseeing, you should always buy a multiday ticket. The extra days are also significantly discounted.

With a multiday ticket, you can use the first day to ride all day long and get familiar with the city and all of its sights and attractions. I would sometimes go around twice if I had the time. The next day, using your knowledge of all the spots you would like to discover, you can go early and essentially use the bus as a taxi to get from your most desired location to the next and so on. It is best to prioritize and pick out a select few areas that you would like to explore.

This worked great in Paris. The second day, I climbed the Eiffel Tower. I also did a lot of window shopping in the fashion district. I loved looking—I've never had that type of clothing and never wanted it, but it is beautiful and exciting to look at.

On my last day in Paris, I decided that my next stop would be Bordeaux and made my room reservations. I had already learned to check for both hostels and Airbnbs.

I decided to spend the last day exploring as well, and as night fell, I was walking back to the hostel while listening to an audiobook on my smartphone, which was in my hip pocket.

Suddenly, the sound stopped. As soon as I realized that silence had settled in, I reached for the phone to see what the problem was. To my complete shock and horror, the phone was gone! Somebody had unplugged the earphones and got away with it within seconds, without me feeling or seeing a thing!

This unexpected turn of events left me completely aghast. I simply couldn't believe what had just happened! All this time, I took comfort in the fact that no one would want my phone since they didn't know my PIN.

Now I know that my password made absolutely no difference—stealing cell phones is a cottage industry in tourist towns, and tourists should be especially aware of their electronics when out and about.

Back at the hostel, I told the clerk of my troubles, and she asked if I wanted to report it to the police. I said yes, and she called up the police station for me. They said that to report phone loss, I had to come to the station and file a report in person.

Pondering over what to do, I wandered around in circles for a while. Reality and common sense began to set in. I realized that reporting would be laborious and time-consuming, and the chances of getting my phone back were next to none.

However, I couldn't travel without my smartphone, and I already had reservations to leave Paris tomorrow. I decided I had only two choices: buy another phone or give up and go home.

When I finally made up my mind, I asked for directions to the nearest electronics shop that sold smartphones.

Bordeaux, France

I love trains. You get to relax while listening to the steady chugging of the carriage and look out the window and see an exciting world beyond.

I even like train stations—cavernous, loud, and busy. The only problem with train stations is that they are frequently located in the city's oldest and most unattractive part. Often, the area is rundown, shabby, and splotched with graffiti. It can give a terrible first impression of the entire town/city.

This was true with Bordeaux. I learned later that a previous mayor made a wonderfully wise decision. He ordered all historic buildings, monuments, and fountains in Bordeaux to be cleaned of centuries of grime. It was one of the cleanest, most beautiful cities I have ever seen. But the train station area was a bit rundown.

I had chosen my accommodation in Bordeaux through Airbnb. My accommodation was slightly removed from downtown but was a delightful one-bedroom apartment, which had a very welcome laundry room.

I rode the city buses quite a bit but walked a lot. Bordeaux is old, beautiful, historical, and known for its wine. It boasts the longest pedestrian mall in Europe. The mall reaches from the college area (relatively inexpensive) to the upscale area (haute couture). I loved strolling and looking through the city, frequenting the cozy sidewalk cafés.

Lyon, France

I was beginning to develop a travel style that was to govern the rest of my trip.

It worked like this: I always arrived in a city with a two-night reservation. In that single day, I decided whether to extend my stay or move on quickly. Usually, I stayed. That involved asking for an extension at the hostel, but I was never denied. Also, I figured that if I had a bad hostel by chance, this allowed me one day to find a better one and move. However, all the hostels I stayed in were lovely, so that never happened either.

In addition, I never knew exactly where I was going next, only the general direction. This was the best part! It enabled me to ask other travelers for advice about locations, hostels, and things to see. They loved being asked and would always answer enthusiastically, in detail.

By doing this regularly, I would often start conversations and get acquainted with people. I found all the most delightful spots that I would never have seen if not for another traveler's recommendation.

From Bordeaux, I wanted to go to Marseille or Monaco, but that is the Riviera. It is an extremely popular spot in which I could not find a bed to reserve. Thus, I settled for Lyon. It was a great alternative. Lyon is a lovely town on the Rhone River and is very hilly.

On my first day in Lyon, I didn't even ask the directions to the downtown area, choosing just to set out and walk. I went in the wrong direction, of course. About a mile (straight uphill), I realized my mistake and went back down. Traveling alone can be pretty lonely sometimes, but this is a perfect example of one of its many advantages. When I make an incredibly foolish mistake, such as the one I just mentioned, I can grin at myself, shake my head, and move on. I can also thank my lucky stars that I wasn't dragging someone else along, so I don't feel guilty the rest of the day.

Lyon's sightseeing bus was not hop-on, hop-off. You bought a ticket, went around once, and that was it. I asked for a tourist information center and, despite thinking I followed the directions to it accurately enough, I couldn't find it. When I did come across it, it was closed.

Later, in a pharmacy, when I asked the clerk for a smaller tube of toothpaste than he had on the shelf (because I was traveling and didn't want to carry a big one), he went in the back and brought back a handful of samples of my brand. No charge! This sweet gesture warmed my heart, and I shared my woes of finding the tourist information center closed.

The clerk wrinkled his forehead in confusion and said, "It can't be! Come over here. I'll point it out for you."

I said, "I was over there at XYZ."

He said, "XYZ is a bank, and this is a Sunday. Of course, it was closed!"

This misstep was, of course, a consequence of my not being acquainted with the local language. Not being able to read the local language is quite disarming, especially for people who are too "whatever it is" (stubborn, dumb, shy) to ask questions. However, I allowed myself to laugh about this mistake. With the clerk's help, I finally found the tourist information center, and indeed it was open.

Lyon proved to be a serene and delightful place to wander in. I liked watching the sunset over the Rhone, glimmering across the buildings with incredible giant murals on the outside. I also found great pleasure in simply walking and looking around, relishing the fact that I was indeed here.

On my last day in Lyon, while in my dorm, I decided to go down to the common room for a cup of coffee. While I was sipping on the hot brew, I had a bright idea. Tomorrow, I would be leaving from the train station. I planned to get to the train station via the tube. However, I previously had not had good luck with finding my way around on the tube and would often end up lost or going in the wrong direction. Thus, I decided I should go out now and scout the way to the train station now so I won't get lost and miss my train tomorrow!

With just an unlimited tube pass and my room key in my pocket, I set out—the wrong way, of course.

After realizing my mistake, I came back and went the right way this time.

Finally, my tube began to approach the rail station, but I ended up going one stop too far. So I got off at the very next stop, hoping to find my way back to the station.

Instead of turning around and making my way back from down below, I made the mistake of going street level. I crossed the street and tried to go back into the tube going the other direction, but my pass was refused. I learned later that unusual behavior causes the system to disable your pass as a way to overcome nefarious cheating schemes. If you do something strange or illogical, the system disables your pass.

Here I was, no money, no identification, no language (I'm in the suburbs, so there is little spoken English), and a useless tube pass. It was definitely time to get over my hesitancy to ask for help!

There was a pizza shop nearby, so I went inside and blabbered my story to the clerk. He didn't understand and looked utterly rattled, but a customer's eyes lit up with understanding, and she spoke up. This lady, in broken English, told me that she loved Americans. She explained that when she was nine years old, her father took her and her sister on a trip to America. Everyone was so friendly to them that she remembered this trip all those years later and had great love and admiration for Americans ever since.

After explaining this to me, she loaded me in her car and took me back to the hostel. Thank goodness my room key had the address. I wouldn't even have known that. Before the evening was over, this sweet lady mentioned that she owned a six-bedroom rental property on the Riviera, and my friends and I were welcome to stay there for free any time. How about that? I found myself silently thanking every single American who was nice to that family forty or fifty years ago.

CHAPTER 3

June 16, 2017

Until now, you've read about my life and the series of events that led me to this adventure.

You might even be wondering how I am doing in that regard. Let me tell you. That wound is still boiling and all-consuming. It is always there. I am swamped, and I am trying hard to ignore it. I don't allow myself time or privacy enough to cry. When I think about it, it hurts too much to breath. This is why people call it heartbreak.

In a way, I could be seen as running away from my problems, but then again, it was near impossible to deal with it without taking a step back and assessing where I stand currently. That's the thing about life, when you're in the thick of it, it just seems too overwhelming to cope with; but when you take a step back, things come into better perspective, and sometimes you are better able to deal with it.

When I left Lyon, I decided to go to Venice. Where Leon was a sleepy city with small towns and villages, quite unlike the city of love, Venice was bustling with life. There were always couples on vacation and those with a nomadic disposition, who chose to come to this beautiful city, both to lose and to find themselves.

The train to Venice goes through Switzerland. The scenery was so breathtaking I couldn't even begin to describe it. There were luscious green hills and lakes as blue as the sky, glimmering in the sun. The houses were built in harmony with nature, they looked like small doll houses from high above. I imagined living in one of those; it had been one of my dreams to live close to nature.

I was in a four-seat car and had coincidentally been lucky enough to get the window seat.

Three young men took the other three seats, I presumed they were friends from the way they were sat comfortably together. They were having fun; I didn't know how to join their conversation, so I continued looking out the window.

The young man next to me exclaimed, "Hey, is that the Matterhorn?"

The others said, "Nah! Couldn't be."

I took this opportunity to participate and said, "It's good enough for me. I'll take it."

They looked it up on their smartphones, and sure enough, it was the Matterhorn.

That broke the ice instantly. They revealed that they were recent graduates of the University of Florida.

They were the sweetest, nicest young men you could find anywhere. Jack told me he had worked in Obama's election campaign. Someday in the future, I will hear that Jack had decided to run for president. I will see his campaign posters everywhere and remember that day on the train. Gordon had been accepted to do his graduate degree in China. He was so excited about that. We bonded so well over the course of that short trip.

I had to change trains in Milan, but I had decided not to stay there because John and I had a wonderful Christmas week there once, so I was avoiding it for reasons you already know. When we got to Milan, my new friends found my connection and carried my bag up and down and up all those stairs. They would have carried me too if I had let them. I sure hated having to part with those guys, and it was all because I had gathered the nerve to speak one sentence. We still keep in touch, as acquaintances often do.

Venice, Italy

As I mentioned before, when I began this adventure, I did not know how to use my smartphone. I could reserve hostels and listen to audiobooks and make WhatsApp calls, and that was all. No Google Maps (online or offline), no looking up anything. I didn't even understand the concept of data. I watched in amazement as my fellow travelers found the answer to any question at any time.

I had decided that it was time for me to start walking from the train stations to the hostels instead of taking a taxi. I had a reason to keep extremely busy and also to save money. Honestly, the main reason was that I knew everyone else was doing it, and I hated to admit that I couldn't. The hostel web pages give directions and told us how far it was, but I couldn't access that data on travel day because I wasn't online. So I got smart and started copying the information into a notebook to reference it when I needed it. If others can follow those directions and walk, then I can too! Maybe not as fast or as directly, but I could do it!

I was wandering around some very dark streets in Venice, very lost, when I saw some other travelers, smartphone held out in front of them like a divining rod and striding confidently. This was *it*! This has got to stop! For goodness' sake, Joy! Ask for help! I did just that. They led me directly to our hostel and spent the next few days teaching me how to use Google Maps online and offline and take a screenshot (oh, wonder of wonders! Manna from heaven! I could finally discard my notebook!). They also shared multiple travelers' apps to make life on the road so much easier and more fun. I continued to learn the whole summer, but this is where it began. And it began because I was staying in hostels where there were lots of friendly people, and I had asked for help. I know now that nobody ever really likes you until you let them help you.

I was beginning to recover from my debilitating shyness. I was recovering because I had to! I learned then that it had been my own reluctance to reach out to people and be close to them that had acted as a barrier. I discovered the importance of challenging myself and going outside my comfort zone.

Venice was also my introduction to a mixed dorm. It was all that was available, and so with no other choice, I decided that if others could do it, then it was something I had to experience too. I mentioned earlier that I liked hostels because they were little communities of their own. People from all parts of the world meeting each other, sharing stories, and learning to like each other.

At every hostel, somebody taught me something new, how to use another feature on the smartphone, a wonderful spot that I must not miss, how to maneuver your visit to this city or that, and their favorite hostels. I felt I had struggled with navigating my way around the country before that, but now it just seemed to make so much more sense. People are always kinder than you expect once you give them an opportunity to genuinely share how they're feeling.

At this particular hostel, a young man from Australia (traveling with his sister) taught me to put vegemite on my toast. He wouldn't travel without it. Some hostels serve breakfast, but all provide a kitchen area where you can make your own. The kitchen area was the best place to socialize, you could be in the middle of microwaving your grilled cheese and you'd see someone struggling to make coffee. So you help each other, and that would start a conversation.

I met many people in the kitchens. There was one girl who ate lots of instant food. She left little packets of ramen and microwavable meals all over the kitchen counter. She persuaded me to try her favorite tinned salmon brand. Surprisingly, I loved it, but mostly I liked the social time in the kitchens.

For the remainder of my trip, I used mixed dorms. It didn't take a lot of getting used to. People didn't walk around shirtless very much, and they were very respectful of each other's spaces. Sometimes we'd have little parties in the lounge area, with large boxes of Italian pizza or even home-cooked spaghetti and garlic bread.

There were no hostels in downtown Venice because real estate there is too expensive. I was lucky to find a hostel that was located in a nice area of the suburbs. It was a house that had been converted into a temporary stay. There were a series of instructions pinned on the wall of the hostel common room for tourists like myself. There was no guide, so we relied on each other for advice and little tricks that could help navigate the place.

- Take the water taxi; It is public transportation. Privately owned boats can be very expensive.
- Get there early. By noon the Piazza San Marco will be so crowded that you cannot see a thing.
- Do not buy even a coke in Piazza San Marco. It will cost you breakfast, lunch, and dinner.
- Go inside Saint Mark's Cathedral.

After I read these instructions, I followed them diligently. I had to be stern to avoid the private boats, but the water taxi (public transport) was delightful. I was in the Piazza (Plaza) by 9:00 a.m., and it was just the pigeons and me. Venice seemed disconcertingly quiet at that time. There was no hustle and bustle of tourists and boats going back and forth. Only stillness with the water glimmering beneath the sun. The beauty of Saint Mark's Cathedral was breathtaking, both from the outside and the inside. The history that the place held was overwhelming to me. There is no point in my repeating all of it, even if I could. All I remember is that a zillion columns cover the front of the cathedral, and each one is made of a different kind of marble.

I walked the streets and waited on the bridges for a gondola to go under, to listen to the gondoliers sing to the lovers in the boats. I would never ride one of those alone. I would have cried the whole way.

I took a tour of the islands and visited Venetian glass factories. The bright colors of the glass are dazzling. They make it into all sorts of décor, lamps, and jewelry. In the evening, instead of the express water taxi to my bus stop, I took a local that went to all the small streets and neighborhoods. I got to watch the people that make Venice work go home to their families.

I wanted immediately to share the experience with my whole family so I called my sister-in-law, using the WhatsApp that she had taught me and told her all about it.

Innsbruck, Austria

When I left Venice, I had decided to go to Innsbruck, Austria. That required that I change trains in Verona, but I couldn't understand the announcements and, of course, didn't ask anyone to alert me, so I didn't get off in Verona. I went all the way to Milan. Still using my rail pass, I tried to get on another train to go back to Verona and get it right this time, but that caused an awful fuss. When things get bad, I pretended to be very dumb and helpless. It's really not a pretense. They usually do what I want to get rid of me. To all the tourists who find the people in Europe to be short-tempered with tourists: I am the reason.

Much later, back home in America, when I was telling some ladies about my travels, one of them said, "I could never do that! I'd be afraid." I asked what exactly she would be afraid of. She said, "I'd be afraid I would get lost!" I laughed and laughed. Now *that* was funny. I was lost all summer.

In Innsbruck, I had booked a real hotel. I couldn't believe the reasonable price. I was walking toward it when I got tired. I spotted an outdoor café that seemed to be closed. No people at all, so I took advantage of sitting and double-checked my directions. While I sat there, a group of Asian tourists passed nearby. One man broke from the crowd and ran toward me. He grabbed my smartphone from the table, waved it at me, and talked excitedly, but not in English. I thought I had lost my phone again. I finally understood that he was an executive at the Samsung factory and was very pleased with my new phone. He grinned and waved as he left. I was glad too. It feels good to make someone happy.

When I got to my hotel, I learned why it was so reasonably priced. My room was a one-person room on the very top floor, the ceiling was sloped, and one twin bed was tucked in. I have never seen another hotel room that was designed for just one person. It was nice—all conveniences, but small and just one twin bed. When I looked out the window, the Alps were touchable. While in that happy little room, I watched the TV news of a terror attack in London and a terrible fire in a tall residential building. I would say an apartment building, but the British call them flats, and a flat building doesn't sound right. I stayed in Innsbruck an extra-long time.

From Innsbruck, I took a day trip to the Swarovski Crystal World Museum. It was fabulous. If you are ever there, don't miss it. I also had the best fish dinner ever in Innsbruck at an outside table of some hotel (not mine). I was completely shocked. I was expecting ordinary. From Innsbruck, I planned to go to Mittelberg, Austria, to visit a friend. I asked the hotel clerks how to get there, but it took a while to convince them that it is a town in Austria. They had to research to tell me how to go. It is a very small ski resort on the northern edge of the Alps, and you can't get there from Austria. You have to go to Munich, Germany, and down from there. Even their mail is delivered from Germany.

Mittelberg, Austria

On the way to Mittelberg, I had to change trains in a small town in Germany. While standing on a platform with others, something strange began to happen. The police showed up and seemed to be very interested in the crowd. I was mostly interested in their hats. They were so cute. I took a picture. Later, I sidled up to the lady cop, told her that her hat was cute, and asked if I could take a picture. She said, "No," so I didn't, but I didn't delete anything either.

The train came, and we all headed south toward Austria. Presently, the train stopped. Strange? There is no station here. Soon the cops came tearing through from back to front and later from front to back. On the way back, they had with them one of the ladies I had noticed on the platform. Well, now, that was fun?

The last leg of this journey is a bus since no train goes to Mittelberg. I had been there before, and I recognized when we got to Mittelberg, but I thought one more stop would be closer to my friend's house, but there was no one more stop. I went up to the driver and got hysterical. I didn't want to keep riding to the next village. He stopped and let me off in the middle of nowhere. It is hard not to be lost when you can't understand the announcements and you don't ask for help.

The middle of nowhere had a little café, so I just went in and had dinner. After dinner, I told the waiter my problem. He called his wife from the kitchen because she spoke English. It turns out they are both from somewhere in Eastern Europe, but they run this restaurant in the summertime. I had my friend's phone number, but my phone doesn't work as a phone, when it has no Wi-Fi, is just a device. I have no address. I have been here before, and I can walk from downtown to her house, but I was not downtown. The wife looked my friend up in the phone book, got her address, put me and my bag in her car, and took me there. See! That is how it works. When you ask for help, you find out how nice people are—nothing to be afraid of.

My friend in Mittelberg (Koletta) is from an old, well-respected family. When she got married, her husband chose to take her name rather than let her change. They live in her family home, which is large. The view from the ski-lined deck is spectacular. I have seen these mountains before covered with snow, but this time, they are bright green. I discover that Mittelberg is not just a ski resort. There are hikers everywhere.

Koletta has three grown children, all of whom are in and out regularly. They are all very musical and perform in public a lot. When I visit, I just go with them to wherever they are playing that night. I couldn't be happier. To visit here is like stepping into a fairy tale.

I have a problem, though. My walking shoes were so worn out (are you surprised?) that I threw them away at the last stop. My hostel mates all said, "Don't buy new ones here. Wait, wait, they are so much less expensive in Eastern Europe!" So I arrived in the perfect hiking town with inadequate shoes. I think Koletta was completely disgusted with me. I was disgusted with myself. I promised to come back with appropriate shoes.

Salzburg, Austria, and Zagreb, Croatia

From Mittelberg, I went to Salzburg. This is a tourist town. It is where the story upon which *The Sound of Music* is loosely based occurred and also where the musical was filmed. The Sound of Music tour buses fill up at least ten a day. I took a day trip to a salt mine where I had to sit down on a slide and shoot sixty feet underground. That was the way the miners went to work. That required more courage than I had, but I did it anyway. Someone took pictures as we flew down that slide and then, in the end, tried to sell them to us. I realized I had deliberately left my purse on the bus. I didn't think I would need it, and we were assured it was safe. A very nice man paid for my picture. After we were back to the bus, I tried to pay him back, but he would not hear of it. Life is like that for me. That is why I love people. I sometimes wonder, is it like that for everyone? I sure hope so. I promise to try my best to make it so.

From Salzburg, you can see the mountain where Hitler had his famous hideaway, Eagle's Nest. I took a day trip to a delightful fishing village where the houses cling to the mountainside. Getting there was a beautiful drive, and the last leg was a boat ride across a lake. Sorry, but I can't remember its name. Salzburg itself is charming, and there is a magnificent fortress castle way up on a hill right inside the city.

From Salzburg, I went to Zagreb, Croatia. The train went right through Ljubljana, Slovenia. I was told later that I should have stopped, but I didn't know. I have to save something for next year. Right?

In the east, even the alphabet changes. The signs look even more incomprehensible. Look at Ljubljana again. Make the *j*'s into *i*'s.

Now you can say it. Loob-lee-anna. Another thing about the east is that in every country, someone says, "Yes, we are a European Union member, but at least we still have our own money." That is such a pain for the traveler. I wished they all used Euros.

In Zagreb, the station was, as usual, in a sad part of town. My hostel was nearby and just as sad. I wrote to a friend, "I am in Zagreb. Glad you are not here." I had reserved for a week, and I was already considering leaving early and just cut my losses. The next day, I got directions and walked to town. What a surprise! The way to downtown was through a long, narrow park. It was full of music kiosks, craft stands, ice cream stands, and beer servers (name your happy place). It was mostly deserted in the morning, but on the way home in the evening, it was all filled with music, dancers, dogs, and families. They all seemed so happy. Like they had just gotten their freedom and were not taking it for granted. It was the first city I have fallen in love with as cities go, but it won't be the last! I could *so* live here!

When I arrived downtown Zagreb, my first goal was a shoe store. The clerk spoke to me, and I said shyly, "English?" She broke out in a big grin and said, "Of course! How can I help you?" I was so delighted that I couldn't stop buying shoes.

I like Eastern Europe! Here are some of the reasons:

- The people are friendly. They act like they are genuinely glad you are here.
- English is widely spoken.
- There are not so many tourists.,
- Beautiful, old, historic architecture is in every town . There is music in the parks. Happy people seem to be celebrating being free. It seems they remember when they weren't.
- Prices are very reasonable.
- Opulent fruits and vegetables are available in outdoor markets every day.
- Outdoor cafés offer gorgeous food! I went back to the same café daily for more of that cold cucumber soup. It was to die for!

I love all of Eastern Europe, but Zagreb in particular. After a week here, I found a nicer hostel closer to town and stayed another week.

In the first hostel (it was OK after I learned to love the city), I want to tell you about two things. One is very good and the other, not so good. I'm going to tell the not so good first. One of the young men in the dorm was drunk! I mean, totally drunk all the time. He only came on vacation to lie in bed and be totally drunk. He was not abusive or embarrassing, just unpleasant. All the other guests got together and asked management to remove him. Management didn't have the heart to evict him, so they gave him a private room. That was fine with the rest of us.

The other incident also involved alcohol. And me! My dorm was in the basement, ground-level in the back, and opened to a nice backyard with tables and chairs. One evening, a pretty young American girl with gorgeous red hair said to me, "Joy! I'll go buy a bottle of wine if you help me drink it." No one ever said anything like that to me before! What a novel idea! To sit down with a friend and the intent to finish a whole bottle of wine! I said OK, because I couldn't think of a reason why not.

We sat outside, just the two of us. After about half the bottle, I opened up enough to tell her about the heartbreak I was living with. I sobbed more tears than the wine I drank. She was so wonderfully kind and sympathetic. She said, "It's OK, Joy. Cry a lot. Tears are God's pain pills."

After that evening, I felt like a heavy load had been lifted. I had been holding all that so tightly within. I will always love that girl. Her name was Emily, and the next day, we went to the town and ate pancakes together.

Up until then, when anyone asked why I was traveling, I told them my whole sad story. People were always very kind and sympathetic, but after this evening, I realized that it was a downer, and it would be better if I did not tell everyone. That was a milestone. After that, I would go weeks without talking about it and sometimes days without thinking about it. Healing had begun.

One day, I called my sister-in-law in Northern Ireland and said, "I plan to be in Dubrovnik in about three weeks. Why don't you and Tom join me there for as long as you can stay?" I couldn't believe it when, a day later, she texted, "We'll be there!" and included a one-week schedule. I knew they were coming partly to check on me and my crazy adventure, but I was delighted that they cared enough to do that. I went directly to a tourist agent and asked her to find a nice hotel in Dubrovnik and reserve it for a week. These are not hostel people.

I heard about a day trip from Zagreb to some beautiful waterfalls called Plitvice Lakes National Park.

I looked at a map and found that it was about halfway to Split, where I planned to go next. I couldn't see the point in going there and coming back, so I booked a hostel and took a bus to Plitvice Lakes.

Plitvice Lakes, Croatia

The hostel in Plitvice was especially nice. A sign just inside the front door said, "Take off your shoes and keep this place clean!" So I did! There were about thirty pairs of shoes on that landing. The environment was especially friendly. Everyone was sitting around tables in the common room, some playing games, and some just sharing stories. They were daring each other to tell their scariest travel stories.

A bus picked us up the next morning and took us to the park. I have seen all of the world's biggest and most famous waterfalls, but Plitvice Lakes waterfalls are the most beautiful I have ever seen. They seem otherworldly. Some cliffs have vegetation and water, not falling from the top as you expect, but just shooting out from various points all over the face of the cliffs.

The next morning, as I was checking out and asking how to get the bus to Split, a fellow hosteler overheard and said, "I am going to Split, and I have a car. Want a ride?" Well, of course! He took me to downtown Split. He was from the Netherlands. He was recovering from a divorce, and his father had loaned him a car for the summer. Smart Dad.

buddies from Florida

A zillion columns

Venetian street scene

View from Kolettas deck

I like this picture because you can't see my shoes

Emily and pancakes

Zagreb

Zagreb markket

Keep this place clean

Scarry stories

Plitvice Lakes

Plitvice Lakes

Plitvice Lakes

CHAPTER 4

Split, Croatia

Split is mind-blowing, with a long and complicated history behind all the quaint architecture. The massive Diocletian Palace is in just the right state of decay—miles of tangled alleyways with a surprise around every corner. Much of *Game of Thrones* was filmed here. The palace is named after Diocletian, a Roman emperor who was a persecutor of Christianity. After he died and Christianity was made legal, many Christian squatters got even by building their homes inside the emperor's abandoned palace. They followed no regulations or plans and built their homes absolutely everywhere, even against or over another house. The area is brimming with pure chaos.

I had a reservation at a hostel called Al's Place, but there were no street names or numbers to guide me. After some searching, I found a red door that I thought might be it, but it only opened into a stairwell. I knew I couldn't pull my giant suitcase around in these cobbled alleys while I hunted for Al's Place, so I left it inside the red door at the foot of the stairs and resumed the search for my hostel.

After inquiring at several pubs, I found Al's Place. I was slowly getting used to asking for help. I went back for my bag (thankfully right where I left it) and checked in.

My dorm was on the second floor, but the chaos in Split seeped in through the walls as well. The buildings are all just thrown together with no plan, no style except chaos. There were no straight lines and no square corners. The window in my dorm opened directly onto the neighbors' patio. The patio was high, about two feet above my floor level (and remember, I was on the second floor).

One evening, when all my dorm-mates had gone out, and I was settled in bed for the night, suddenly a party on the patio next door broke into full swing. Split is a party town, alive and pulsing with unrestrained energy. I opened my bleary eyes in confusion and stumbled out of bed—I was now awake, so I thought I may as well go to the bathroom.

The people on the patio noticed my shuffling footsteps and started fumbling with the window, trying to shut it. They seemed embarrassed, as if they didn't want to disturb anyone. Amid this commotion, I stepped toward the window and said, "Don't bother. You are on holiday. Have your fun."

A person from the patio asked, "Would you like a drink?"

My half-asleep brain erupted in a frenzy. *Of course not! Old ladies do not drink in the middle of the night!* However, the party seemed to be in good spirits and the people, cherry and friendly. Aloud I said, "Sure."

"Why don't you join us?" he said as he handed me the drink.

Alarm bells began to blare through my head. *Are you out of your mind? I have on my pajamas! What kind of person do you take me for* ? However, the ringing laughter of the party-goers and the steady rhythm of the music enticed me completely, and I said "OK."

They pulled me up through the window. I sat in one spot, and throughout the night, every single one of those young people came and sat beside me, introduced themselves, and chatted until someone else demanded their seat. I met so many interesting individuals. One guy was a fireman who had fought in London's big apartment house fire that I mentioned earlier. Those guys were all from England, and they had anecdotes and stories that left me absolutely riveted! We partied till the sun came up. This remains one of my most treasured memories.

In my remaining days, I spent my time exploring the streets of Split. There were lots of noisy birds in the old castle rafters.

Along the outside of the walls, there was a sea of outdoor stalls that sold everything from holiday clothes to silly gadgets that made frog croaking noises. A small sum could also get you twenty minutes inside a 3D headset where you could meet the Roman who built this palace. The same Roman will then take you on a tour, proudly showing off his palace as it was when it was new.

Dubrovnik, Croatia

After I had all the fun I could have in Split, I took a bus to Dubrovnik. As the bus drove down the coast, we halted at a spot where everybody had to get off and show your passport. That was because we were now entering Bosnia. Bosnia is about ten minutes wide, and then, after another showing of passports, you are back in Croatia. It looks like Bosnia wanted a seaport, and they got exactly that—just a little neck crosses Croatia that reaches the Adriatic Sea.

I had a hostel reserved in Dubrovnik. My relatives were coming next week, and we will all stay in a nice hotel. However, until then, I will stay in a hostel. My hostel had a huge deck with a view of the water where you could watch all the cruise ships coming and going. This hostel is especially charming, and it has a happy hour on the house every day at 6:00 p.m.

Dubrovnik is larger than Split, more preserved, and yes, more beautiful; but it lacked Split's dynamic and fast-paced nature. The cruise ships come and go with regularity. The crowd of tourists is also older. It takes a day to see Dubrovnik, and then, for me, it is all over. My hostel mates (they were young, the older crowd I mentioned was from the cruise ships) were doing bungee jumping, sky diving, and taking part in other daredevil stunts, but that was not for me.

While out exploring, I found a small bar clinging to the outside, but near the top of the city wall. Access was from the top of the wall, so you had to climb downward to the bar. Once there, you could sit and drink lemon beer and watch the divers jump, with great bravado, into the brilliant blue Adriatic Sea. Sitting at this bar was a lovely way to spend an afternoon. However, they had a secret to keep people from occupying a seat all day. It was hard to get in and out of that bar, and it had no bathroom.

I met a young man in Dubrovnik who had unfortunately been robbed. He didn't ask for money, and he said that he had wired home for help; however, I noticed that he wasn't eating, so I gave him enough money to eat for a week. He was overwhelmed. I told him it was because people were always so kind to me that I found joy in giving back. I sincerely hope that he overcame that adversity and continued to travel.

Since Dubrovnik is great but not quite compelling enough for a whole week's entertainment, I began to worry about what to do with my relatives when they came. Rats! I wish I had asked them to come to Split instead—but I had already paid for this hotel in Dubrovnik. Slowly, I began to formulate a plan. I would keep this hotel but splurge for two nights in Split in the middle of the week. We could take the ferry up the coast and back, which I would have liked to do anyway. The ferry stops at multiple islands and floats above that gorgeous deep, blue Adriatic Sea. I got on the internet and could find no fancy hotels in Split, but there was something billed as a luxury apartment. I booked it for two nights.

On the day Tom and Jackie came, I was delighted. Everything was meticulously planned and perfect. We had a great two days in Dubrovnik and then split for Split. (Sorry. You must have known I'd do that eventually.) The ferry ride was almost surreal—we just floated through those idyllic islands and bright blue waters.

Split Again

We arrived in Split at the ferry terminal, which required that we walk through the palace and the best of Split. As we walked toward our location, the streets began to grow dark and hot. Croatia in July is scorching! Once again, I had to deal with the lack of streetlamps and signs. We found a building that seemed to match our directions, but it was dark, unmarked. Still, we opened the heavy doors and went in. There was no receptionist. It was just a grimy, unfurnished landing area. The two side doors were locked, so I shouted up the stairs but received only an echo in reply. To say that I was frightened at this point is a vast understatement. Alone, I believed that I could cope with anything, but I had Tom and Jackie in my care. My terror began to grow and became obvious. Noticing my anxiety, Tom went back outside and walked around the building. He said he saw some lights on in the basement, and he saw bunk beds! Horrors!

As a last-ditch effort, we all shouted up the stairs. This time, a young girl came creeping down. I showed her my reservation. She said, "Oh yes. It is up here." We followed her. At this point, I was hoping for anything, even the bare minimum. I whined, "I hope luxury means air-conditioned?" Upstairs and down a long narrow hallway, you'll never guess what we found. An actual luxury apartment! I had never been so relieved in my life. I was hysterical. I giggled the rest of the evening.

Split was a joy to visit, and my guests liked it as much as I did.

Dubrovnik Again

The ferry back to Dubrovnik was like gliding through paradise again. We walked around the top of the Dubrovnik city wall. It was hot and rugged. Not an easy trip! Yet the view of the old city was worth it. As recently as 1992, Dubrovnik was attacked by the Yugoslav Army in an attempt to detach this part of Croatia and add it to their empire. From the vantage point of the wall, you can clearly see which part of the city had been burned because the newer roof tiles are a slightly different color.

Split. This man translated the Bible into Croatian.

Split. Just the right amount of decay

Split. Little winding alleys everywhere!

Split

Split. More alleys

Split. Sometimes you get a surprise

notice the little tiny garbage truck in the background

Split

Look! He dumps into the big one

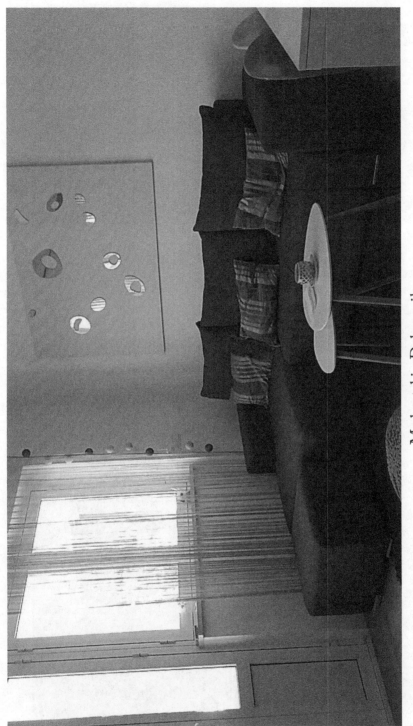

My hostel in Dubrovnik

View from My hostel in Dubrovnik

View from My hostel in Dubrovnik

The Dubrovnik wall

Lemon Beer

Jumpers

CHAPTER 5

Kotor, Montenegro

In the morning, my guests were to take a bus to the airport while I had plans to continue my travels. I checked the schedule and found a bus to Kotor, Montenegro, which departed thirty minutes later.

The reason I was traveling to Kotor was that another hosteler had enthusiastically suggested that I should. I had never even heard of Montenegro before, never mind Kotor, but I decided to travel there and experience this new place.

We all went to the bus station together. After my family's bus arrived and they departed for the airport, I learned that the bus to Kotor was sold out. There was now a seven-hour wait for the next bus. Though the wait was long, I didn't mind because I was alone once again, and with no one else to be concerned about, I knew that I could cope with anything!

Late afternoon, I got on my bus only to discover that my assigned seat was next to a local who smelled so bad that it wasn't just irritating; it actually hurt the inside of my nose. As soon as I spotted an empty seat, I immediately hurried to it. However, I was granted only a few minutes of relief, as when the lady assigned to that seat came looking for it, she made me go right back. The trip to Kotor was starting to seem quite long. Fortunately, the offending local did not go all the way to Kotor.

The big bus drove onto a wooden raft just as the sun was setting, and we ferried across a lake. I thought that was a rather different experience. I watched the whole operation closely, hoping all the while for no high wind gusts.

When we finally arrived at Kotor, it was magical. There were buildings up the side of a mountain that looked vertical to me. Since it was nighttime, you could see glimmering lights all over the mountainside—the view looked like it was straight out of a dream. There was also a giant rag doll to greet us.

When I got off the bus, I hurried to find a bathroom. I can read *toylet* in any language, and it was not long before I found one. However, to my utter disdain, a man was sitting at the door to collect money. I tried to desperately explain my situation to this man, hoping he would be considerate. "Are you kidding? I just got here, and I don't have any of your money! No, I can't go get any right now! I'll pay when I come out!"

He probably understood none of that, but at least he didn't chase me down or refuse entry. In a few minutes, I heard another lady have the same conversation. She came in grumbling, and we struck up a conversation. She was the same lady who wouldn't let me steal her seat! During our conversation, she explained that she was from Austin, Texas, where I once lived. Coincidentally, she only lived about two blocks from my old house. Her husband is a professor at the University of Texas. Both of them were in their seventies, and they traveled like this (hostel hopping) a lot. Well, hallelujah! If I am crazy to love traveling like this, then at least I am not alone.

We decided to share a taxi. First, we went to my hostel, but the couple refused to leave until they knew I had checked in safely. It turned out that my hostel had a waterline break, and so the management was sending all the guests to another hostel, which just so happened to be the one where my new friends were staying. These two wonderful people, and their taxi was waiting for me the whole time when this news was broken to me. We all proceeded to their hostel and checked in.

Kotor was another fascinating, old village. I explored the city and would frequently share dinner and wine with my new friends for two days. They had plans to head to Greece later, but I didn't want to go to Greece for the same reason I didn't want to stay in Milan. However, their very next stop was Tirana, Albania, and that sounded like a wonderful idea.

Tirana, Albania

The bus to Tirana was uneventful. The only thing I remember is that I could not recognize the growing crops along the way. Being a farm girl, I could spot and name almost everything that grows in North America. I learned later that this crop was marijuana, but I hadn't seen it before.

In Tirana, we took a taxi to the hostel. My new friend had made the reservations, so I was a bit out of the loop. The taxi left us in front of a hostel, but somebody said "No. This is not it."

Our hostel was down a nearby alley. While walking to it, we encountered a tremendous amount of clutter and scrap clogging up the pathway. After trudging through all this, we came upon a stairway with crumbling cement. We went up the stairs and arrived at a very comfortable, homelike hostel.

The Albanians had just deposed a dictator about ten years ago. Our host assured us that Albania loves America more than any other country in Europe. For the second time, I was told that somebody loves Americans.

The hostel we were staying at was run by two ambitious brothers who wanted to be capitalists. They both had full-time jobs but adjusted their shifts so one of them could always be at the hostel.

The kitchen was too small to allow self-service, so you had to sit at a small table (three at a time, no more), and the host would make your breakfast and set it in front of you. It was the best hostel breakfast I had had anywhere. When the housekeeping lady showed up, the host introduced her as Mom. They directed us to the best sightseeing route.

We saw the old communist headquarters and walked in a park where the public was not allowed during the communist era and the dictatorship. There, we saw a giant glass pyramid that the dictator's son-in-law had built as a monument to his father-in-law. All the glass was shattered, as high as a human could throw a rock.

Later, we found a new fish market with an attached open market area. We sat during the heat of the day, drinking unlimited cold beer, and enjoying at least ten fresh seafood dishes. The total bill was twelve euros. For all three of us!

The second (and last) evening, we walked to the fish market again for dinner. We sat and exchanged stories until almost midnight. When we arrived back at the hostel, I discovered that I had left my phone lying on the table at that same restaurant, which was about six blocks away from us. There were no taxis to be found this late. I tried to convince my friends that if I went alone, I could walk faster, but they wouldn't hear of it. I walked very fast, and they kept up. The restaurant was closed when we got there, but the waiter was standing right there with my phone, waiting for us to return.

This American loves Albania!

Welcome to Kotor

Charm of Kotor

Brooms

New apartments facing the Tirana market

The market

CHAPTER 6

Sofia, Bulgaria

My first EU rail pass had been used up some time ago, and I was taking a break before activating the next one. Bus service was vastly better in the East, anyway.

I was by myself once again, since my friends from Texas had gone south to Greece.

I thus began to plan the remainder of my travels. I looked at a map for my next stop and decided I wanted to travel to Sofia, Bulgaria. However, that was too far for a one-day bus journey. My concerns were quickly taken care of, though, as I had a convenient app called Rome2Rio that made planning travel easy. You just had to tell it you want to go from place A to place B, and it would map out all the ways to get there, including the cost of travel and time.

In hindsight, I should have told Rome2Rio that I wanted to go to Sofia—it would have made things so much simpler. Instead, I looked at a map, picked a mid-distance city (Skopje, pronounced skoop-ee-a, in Macedonia), and told Rome2Rio I wanted to go there.

After the app provided me with the needed instructions, I bought a ticket and set out. The problem was that no bus went directly to Skopje. So I had to detour to Pristina, Kosovo, and then head over to Skopje. I stayed just one night there and continued to Sofia the next day- my actual destination! The first leg of this day's journey took me all the way back to Pristina, Kosovo, and then on to Sofia. I wasted about six hours backtracking simply because I didn't ask the right question.

In Sofia, I had booked a hostel that had been recommended and spoken highly of by many other hostelers. It was *the* place to be in Sofia, named Hostel Mostel. Hostels are notoriously hard to find, and this one was deviously well-hidden.

Sofia was one of the spots where I refused to hire a taxi, so I walked toward the hostel for hours. Once it was found, though, I realized the place was well worth the trouble. It was big, homey, friendly, and they served breakfast *and* dinner. They also organized a lot of activities, making it a worthwhile experience.

On the first day, I went on a walking tour led by a friendly tour guide who provided fascinating information about the city. Throughout the tour, I discovered that Sofia had been inhabited since at least 7000 BC. It was populated because it had an abundance of freshwater springs, which were all over town.

One of Sofia's most fascinating characteristics was that its people were excavating their history right beneath their feet. There were numerous places throughout the city where you could enter the archaeological dig area, which was extensive and well-lit by glass domes at street level. These engaging historic spots were totally free to explore, and the digging continued.

Constantine was the Roman emperor who declared Christianity to be the official religion of Rome. His mother was from Sofia. He tried to get Sofia to be the capital instead of Rome, but that didn't fly. However, he built a small church here to honor his mother. It is the oldest church in the world to still have its original roof.

When the communists were in power, they were destroying all the churches. To protect this very church, the Sofians built tall buildings around it so it couldn't be seen.

A modern politician had also built a statue honoring Saint Sofia, which was placed downtown. However, the educated folk resented it greatly since this city, named Sofia, was standing here long before the saint's arrival—before Christ was even born.

Our tour guide told us that although Bulgaria was allied with Hitler in WWII, they were the only country to save 100 percent of their Jewish population. It appears the Bulgarians were good at procrastination. Hitler had told them to send their Jews, but they replied that their railways were closed for repair, and they would comply as soon as the RR was fixed. Then they ordered the Jews to restore the RR, which of course, did not need fixing. Thus, the Jewish population was able to remain in Bulgaria safely.

The next day, our tour group took a day trip to a working monastery up in the mountains. Before the monastery, our guide took us to a holy spot situated even higher on the mountain. This was where the hermit monk, to whom the monastery was dedicated, first came. We saw the cave where he lived alone for many years. It had a rear escape, which meant crawling up through a claustrophobic little tunnel, which I did not like.

I could barely keep up with the rest of my group, but I kept going anyway until I realized everyone else had been out of sight for some time. The tour guide finally came back for me, as he knew I was still back there. The trek was a circular route, and the others were back at the van. When we got back to the van, all the people were extremely kind and understanding. I don't think they minded waiting for me at all.

The monastery was large, beautiful, and enjoyable. I usually do not buy souvenirs because I don't have room and don't need the weight. Yet at this place, I gave in to my urges to buy something for myself, and you would never guess what I bought—an egg! An empty, intricately painted eggshell. I knew it would be nearly impossible to get home without breaking it, but I decided that I was willing to give it a try. Thankfully, it did get home safely.

On one of my final days in Sofia, while I was exploring their archaeological digs alone, I met a lady from London who was also traveling by herself. Remarkably, she was in a wheelchair but hadn't let that stop her. Indeed, if you want to travel, nothing can get in your way.

Sofia is the second city I have declared a love affair with. Still eastward bound, I booked an overnight express train for Istanbul, Turkey.

Church with original roof

Sofia. The glass domes allow light into the digs below

Sofia's history. This is where I met the lady in the wheel chair

An active monastary in the mountains above Sofia

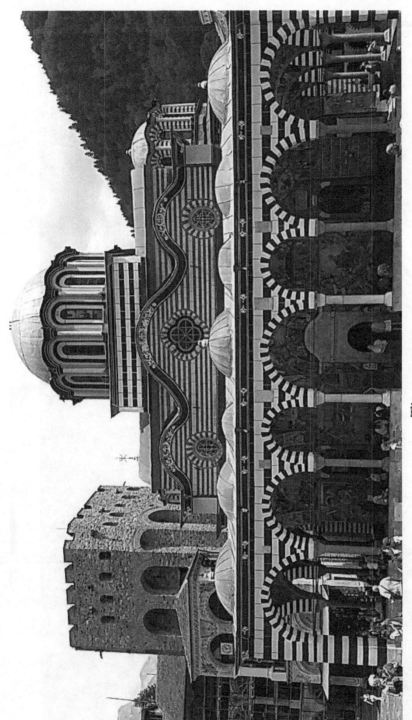

The monastary

The monastary

Sofia. Hostel Mostel

Sofia. Hostel Mostel

CHAPTER 7

Istanbul, Turkey

It was now time to activate my second EU rail pass and begin my journey to Turkey.

The train to Istanbul was a sleeper, but we were awakened suddenly and herded out of the train in the middle of the night. We stood in line, bleary-eyed, in an unfurnished, dimly lit, mosquito-infested shed. This was Turkish Immigration control. The process to verify our identities took about an hour.

Back on the train, after moving for a short while, we stopped and went through the entire process again. I was told why there were two checks, but currently, I don't remember the reason.

I stayed awake after the second time because dawn was breaking, and views of Turkey were spreading across my window. I saw large buildings up on the hillsides, bathed in soft yellow light. They were obviously residence buildings but were quite far removed from the cities. I wondered what all the people who resided in these buildings did for a living?

The buildings were similar to others I had seen in Eastern Europe. They were utterly square and plain. The tour guides always apologized for them and said they were leftovers from the communist era. I guess many people needed someplace to live, and so these buildings were built, and that was indeed commendable, but a little more attention to aesthetics could have gone a long way.

Trains do not go into Istanbul as the city is too old and fragile. Adding an entire rail infrastructure could ruin it. Thus, our train halted well outside the city, and we boarded a bus for the remainder of the trip. The bus followed a road that ran just outside the city wall. The wall was old and unbelievably still standing—the longest and highest wall I had seen in any ancient city! It made me want to call the capital Constantinople once again.

From the bus station, I took a taxi to my hostel. This was a good decision because I would have never found that hostel on my own. The streets in Istanbul are exceedingly narrow and tangled, and most of the old areas allow no auto traffic at all. The taxi had to drive a long way, but I was glad I had taken it as I would never have found that hostel unaided. While I was there, I learned the area, and on leaving day, I walked to the bus station, discovering that it wasn't very far.

At the hostel, I had my first experience with ageism.

As usual, I had reserved a dorm, but they insisted that their fine print stated no one over forty could stay in a dorm. I never read the small print. They said I could upgrade to a private room, or they could refund my deposit and I could stay elsewhere.

I explained that I immensely enjoyed dorms and had stayed in them multiple times, but there was no budging. So I chose the upgrade and stayed in a private room.

I was told later that my room cost less than half of what it would have two years ago. It seems as if Istanbul used to be booming, but the failed coup last year had scared away the tourists.

The receptionist was on the second floor, my room was on the third, and the common area was up two more levels on the roof. All the stairs were narrow and steep but climbing them proved to be worth the effort. The roof offered a fantastic view, allowing you to see across the Bosporus Strait and into Asia!

Venturing outside in Istanbul was very different from anything I had experienced before. Every shopkeeper came out to accost you. They pleaded and followed you down the street. Sometimes you could accumulate a group of five or six pleading with you to purchase their wares. They would say, "Come over here. It's a museum, and it's free!" But it was just their shop, of course.

There were hundreds of carpet shops. If you ever went in, they would unroll carpets before you until you made them stop. It was pretty embarrassing when the shopkeepers would go through that ordeal while you intended to get out without buying! The shopkeepers didn't touch, but they indeed invaded your personal space. It was most uncomfortable. I learned to buy guided tours because the guides would protect me to some degree. However, some of the tours included a trip to a carpet shop. I just waited outside.

The Blue Mosque is breathtaking from both inside and out. The courtyard is finished with marble and is so expansive that the Romans used to hold chariot races there. Nothing of the sort can take place there now, as there are monuments, statues, and obelisks all over the place. On this day, I had on pants and a sleeveless top. This meant I had to cover up my "indecency" with the help of two big scarfs before I could enter the mosque.

Hagia Sophia is a former Greek Orthodox cathedral built in AD 537. It is famous for its massive dome and detailed mosaics of Biblical scenes. When Turkey conquered Constantinople, they converted this cathedral to a mosque. Only recently has it been restored back to its original state of being. However, churches are not allowed in Turkey, therefore it is now referred to as a museum.

I also toured a large center from which the Ottoman Empire was administered, which was now a museum with many relics of The Prophet. It contained his razor, his hair cuttings, and more. One spot had a man reading from the Koran where the recitation had been going on continually for generations.

On the second evening of my stay, there was a storm with copious amounts of rain, wind, and hail. It was exciting to watch from the roof of the hostel but bad enough to drive us inside shortly.

I had already purchased tours for the following two days, but as we toured, everything we were meant to see was closed because of storm damage. The only thing open for business was the cemetery—at least it was a nice one! The guide bravely tried to soldier on, but the tour was ultimately hopeless. The next day, I went on a full-day cruise of the Bosporus Strait. It was official—I had traveled all the way to Asia.

Many tourists come to Istanbul primarily for the shopping. The Grand Bazaar in Istanbul is one of the largest and oldest covered markets in the world. It is a labyrinth of colorful markets with sixty-one covered streets and over four thousand shops that sell leather, jewelry, and gifts. Mostly, you can find knock-off designer purses and shoes. Some women I met there were tasked with buying up to ten handbags for everyone they knew back home.

A young man at a hostel several cities back told me that he visited a Turkish bath when he was in Istanbul. He enjoying it so much that he went to the bath every single day of his stay! I simply had to see what all the fuss was about.

There were several stages of getting clean and relaxed at the bath, and the people working there didn't rush you. I think I may have been there for three hours. The last stage was sitting with your feet in a tub while little fishes nibbled the dead skin away. It was hard not to twitch, but the fish didn't seem to mind. They would skitter away and then come right back. I definitely enjoyed the experience, but once was enough.

On the way back to the hostel, I tried to take a shortcut but soon realized that there were no other women in sight, and everyone was staring at me. I quickly made my way back to the main road. A woman alone, of any age, is quite an oddity in Istanbul.

I had prepaid for six nights, but after five, I decided to cut my losses and go on my way. I very much enjoyed Istanbul, but I would not go back there alone.

I had heard stories of great things to see in Turkey's inland, but I did not want to travel any further east. I also did not want to go to Greece; therefore, the only way out was to retrace my steps back to Sofia. I was lucky to have seen Istanbul. Just two days after I left, Americans were forbidden to travel there because of some diplomatic dust-up.

My intent was to stay one night in Sofia and move on. I had not booked a hostel because of my decision to leave Istanbul early.

Moreover, I did not want to go back to Hostel Mostel because it was too far from the rail station. When I alighted from the train in Sofia, a man approached me. He said he worked for the railroad, and I spotted an official-looking badge on his person. He stated that his job was to help me in any way he could. I told him I was looking for a hostel, to which he replied by saying he knew a good one nearby. The man then took my bag and led me all the way to the hostel, which was small and even nicer than Hostel Mostel.

The following day, the gentleman met me again and led me all the way back to my new connection. His name was Angel, and he was over sixty-five. He said he loved his job and had been working there for a long time.

His help and service lingered in my mind for a long while, and I still wonder about him. I had never heard of a job like his before. I wondered if the railroad really paid him. If not, he must just live on the tips he earns.

Belgrade, Serbia

My next destination was Belgrade, Serbia. It was a long journey, and when I arrived, darkness had begun to settle. Looking at the surroundings, I opted for a taxi. However, I had an additional problem.

I said to the taxi driver, "I haven't eaten since morning, and it's now painful. Can you find someplace to eat for me?"

He replied, "Sure," and then drove and drove. I knew the place he was taking me was far out of the way since hostels are usually near the train station. At last, he found the place he was looking for and parked in front, mentioning that he would wait for me.

I asked, "Are you going to sit here, or are you coming in?"

He said, "As you wish." Of course, I told him to come in. I just could not be that cold. After settling in, we ordered drinks and then hailed the waiter to order food. The waiter said, "Oh, no! We stopped serving food at 10 pm." We had just missed it!

My taxi driver offered to take me to another place, but I was getting nervous about the time. I was just as tired as I was hungry. I was also getting worried about the large taxi bill I had probably racked up. I said, "Please just take me to my hostel. I am sure I will live to eat another day."

I usually chose my hostels from a list on my app, and it was hard to predict what they would really be like. The hostel I chose in Belgrade was named Home Sweet Home, and it was the nicest one I had ever seen. A slight problem was developing, though. The area was suddenly hit with a record-breaking heatwave, and most hostels did not have air-conditioning. This one had fans at least, which helped considerably. Many hostels didn't even have fans!

At this point, I have a confession to make. I had been on the road for four months now. My passion is old, historic cities, but I had seen so many of them that after a while, they all started to blur together and become increasingly similar. Though Belgrade is a beautiful old town, the truth is that I don't remember it entirely. However, I am sure it was delightful, and if it had been the only city I saw, I would have raved about it forever.

Budapest, Hungary

From Belgrade, I went to Budapest. I was breaking a rule here because this was a place John and I had visited before. Perhaps, it is time to talk about that again. I really had been too busy to contemplate my boiling sore of grief, so looking upon it now revealed a large, sensitive scar. It hurt to even look at it, but the open sore was not boiling anymore. I thought, for the first time, that I may just get through this.

When John and I were in Budapest, it was just a day trip from Vienna. We didn't see much and didn't stay there, so it felt as though perhaps I could stand to explore the city in depth.

Budapest was magnificently beautiful, and I rode a city bus to explore and experience the place thoroughly. I remember many fountains with people playing in them because of the heat—I may have dashed in and out of a few myself!

Though I would love to elaborate in great detail upon the various places I visited and the experiences I had, I would like to take a break from that and describe some all-important lessons I learned through my travels.

The first thing I learned was that the EU rail passes were a bad idea for a whole range of reasons. They are not economically advantageous, and buses and trains are quite inexpensive in the East anyway. The passes actually limit your options. It is far better to compare and choose your mode of transportation based on each individual circumstance. I spoke to other hostelers who had purchased EU rail passes, and they had all come to this very conclusion.

The second thing is that Europe is too big to see in six months. You should decide on a limited area to experience fully and save the rest for another time.

The third thing is that six months is a long, long time. Over time, you get tired and jaded, and you don't enjoy the trip as much as you should.

The last thing is that for this kind of travel, having booked a return is a mistake. It affects the planning of the whole last part of your trip. From now on, I will buy one-way tickets. That way I can go home when (and from any place) I want to.

My new philosophy of traveling and of life is to stop planning and controlling every aspect. Keep your options and possibilities open, and just let life happen. It flows better that way. This approach can be scary at first, but it gets easier with practice. It is best to let go of your tension and fear, as worry never pays off. Worry is just imagination misused. You make up something to be afraid of and then concentrate on it.

During this trip, I had kept a very hectic pace. Though that was by design and for a particular reason, I decided that in the future, I would stay longer in each spot and see each area more thoroughly. It is not necessary to see all the world in one trip.

Krakow, Poland

The hostel in Krakow was very nice and air-conditioned. During my stay there, I met an American man in his late sixties who told me he had gone hostel hopping last year. He enjoyed it so much that he went back home, sold all his belongings, and started living out of his backpack. He said, "I am not going home."

I am not ready for something quite so drastic yet, but the idea intrigued me. The hostel included breakfast and was just nine euros per night. You couldn't maintain a home in America for that.

This man was undoubtedly a fascinating character. He told me that the only problem he faced while living on the road was acquiring his medication. Upon inquiry, he revealed that the medication was for bipolar disorder. I wondered whether that had anything to do with the impulsive decision to totally change his lifestyle.

Next, he said that he was looking for a wife! Later, he told me he had met a woman online who lived in Romania, and they had a Skype date later. After that date was over, he was bouncing all over the place, proclaiming to the world that he had met the woman of his dreams, was in love, and had plans to travel to Romania to get her. He left the very next day, so I can only hope that his life turned out well.

I had come to Krakow because of recommendations from hostelers. I am glad I listened! The old square was beautiful, historical, and fun. It had four or five performing groups at a time and other attractions right in the court. Mostly, there was a whole lot of shopping. Their specialty was amber jewelry.

There were also beautiful horses with buggies for the tourists to ride. The outdoor cafés were plentiful, welcoming, and wonderful.

One of the attractions is the old Jewish quarters. Schindler's factory still stands there. The pharmacy in the ghetto (made famous by a book of the same name) is also present.

However, the biggest attraction at Krakow was the Auschwitz camp. You must not miss that if you come to Krakow. I saw some things there that I just cannot talk about and came away feeling a sense of deep sadness. All these years later, the things that occurred there are still too horrible to imagine! The fact that such terrible acts happened is truly beyond belief. Visiting Auschwitz is a horrendous experience, but you will still be glad you did it. It is now a place where one can honor the memories of all those who lost their lives and a reminder that though humanity's history was bleak and cruel, we must try to never allow something of that caliber to happen again.

Communist blocs. Do you think they are pretty

Istanbul old wall

Bosporus Straits from my hostel roof. That's Asia there

Sidewalk cafe in Istanbul

The blue mosque. Up close

The courtyard where the Roman chariots used to race

Telephone poles in rural USA were like this in my childhood

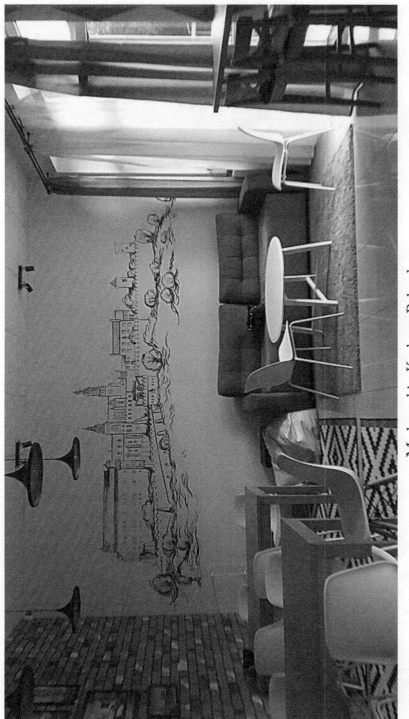

My hostel in Krakow, Poland

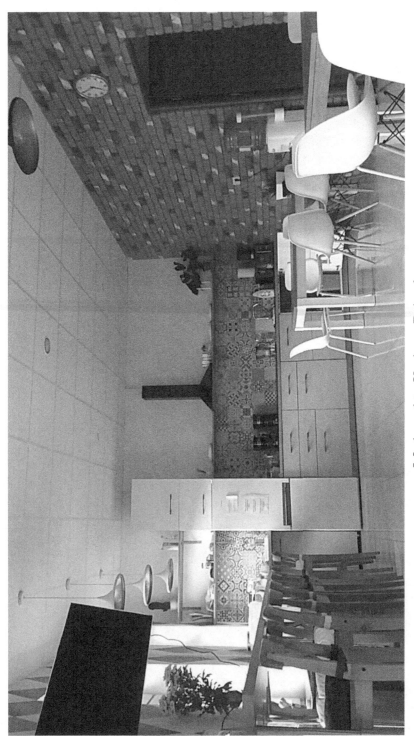

My hostel in Krakow, Poland

Schindler's factory

Break time

Huge market building in middle of an even bigger square. Krakow

Shops inside the market building

Shops inside the market building

Break time

CHAPTER 8

Prague, Czech Republic

Prague is a delightful city set on the Vltava River. Charles bridge is pedestrian only and is crowded with street peddlers. The bridge is totally covered with padlocks put there by lovers to ensure lasting love. The main attraction for me, though, is the architecture. I never get tired of just walking the streets and looking at the houses. Also I ride city buses and drink in the color and shapes.

My hostel has decorated outside with life-sized figures balanced on high wires. When I got ready to leave, I chose to walk to the bus station. Another bad decision. I wandered for hours, but I enjoyed it.

I was going to Český Krumlov, a small village in the south of the Czech Republic, again based on advice from another hosteler.

Český Krumlov, Czech Republic

The times I have followed advice from fellow travelers have all turned out to be great successes. It makes sense! Why would anyone bother to recommend an out of the way place unless it was especially good?

Český Krumlov is a small town again set on the Vltava river, but the river is much smaller at this point than it is in Prague. It is very crooked. Multiple horseshoe bends ensure that most of the town is built right on the river edge. I chanced to land in an especially quaint hostel run by two charming ladies. It is called the Skippy Hostel. The deck literally sticks out over the river.

This river is very popular with tourists for rafting and kayaking. Renting these vessels is a major business here. There are occasional low dams on the river, but each one has a small spot where the boats can pass through. There is one of these dams just upstream from the Skippy Hostel. When the boats pass through, only about half of them make it without turning over. The people always sputter and splash and think they are drowning for a moment and then realize it is only three feet deep, so they just stand up. Now they have to catch their boat, oars, and whatever else, dump the water (which isn't easy), and get organized and back into the boat to continue downstream.

I could sit on that flowered deck and laugh at those frolickers day in and day out. The town itself is historic; it has a magical castle and many other old buildings. It is easy to walk all over this small town and every turn is a delight. But the very best part about Český Krumlov is the people. The proprietors of Skippy Hostel and I bonded, and we talked for hours. Skippy speaks good English but Hana apologized and said she couldn't speak English, but she said enough words to warm my heart.

Skippy, Hana, and another friend, Peter, who plays a mean Spanish guitar, have formed a music group. They play on the streets sometimes but always in a club on the weekends. Skippy is a nickname but now that we are more acquainted I call her by her real name, Zdenicka.

While we talked, I told Zdenicka my sad story of why I was traveling, and she repeated it all to Hana in her language. When I was ready to leave, Hana took me to the rail station in her car. Upon parting Hana struggled for the words, hugged me, and said, "Please come back!" That is all it took for me! Will I go back? You bet! Again and again. The atmosphere there is loving, casual, and perfect.

This chapter is short because, to me, what happened in Český Krumlov is worth its own chapter. Remember when I said that my dream had been to settle somewhere till you knew the locals and then move on? Well, when you have been back to Český Krumlov as many times as I have and come to love Zdenicka, Hana, and many of their friends as much as I do, you have no desire to move on.

My hostel Prague

My hostel Prague

My hostel Prague

My hostel Prague

Prague. My hostel. My feet

Politics Prague style. It hasn't worked. Russia is still threatening Ukraine

Prague. I don't know. It was there so I took its picture

Anything for the tourist

Prague. Charles Bridge. Pedestrian only. Lots of intricate, old statues

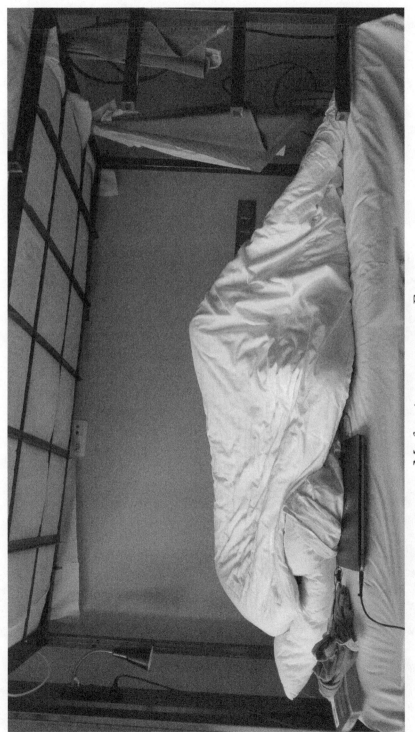

My favorite room-mate. Ever

I got lost on the way to the bus station but I found
this. I really like architecture that is different

Ceske Krumlov

Ceske Krumlov

Ceske Krumlov

View from deck of Skippy Hostel

Zdenicka (Skippy) and Hana

CHAPTER 9

Nuremberg, Germany

On German maps, it is Nurnberg.

On the train to Nuremberg, I met a brother and sister from Pakistan. They were both civil engineers and were working in Germany. She had been promised to marry by her family, but her betrothed told her that he would require that she quit work and stay home, so she ran away and did not marry. The sad part is that her cultural upbringing was so strong that she fell into depression with feelings of having betrayed her family and being unloved and unworthy. Her brother said he approved of what she did. I chimed in with my approval, but I'm afraid it didn't cheer her up much.

The Nuremberg walking tour guide talked a lot about WWII. A lot of Nuremberg's history is that time frame. This is where the famous Nuremberg Trials were held. Also there is a Nazi museum, which is in a building on a giant parade ground. Hitler liked large parades and shows of power. This is where his young Nazi organization held annual conventions. The guide said many young Germans have a sense of guilt about their dark history.

Dresden, Germany

I went to Dresden because it has a nice name, and it was about half way to Berlin, where I really wanted to go. Dresden is extremely impressive. Grand and beautiful. I have been told that Dresden was completely destroyed in the war, but all the old buildings have been rebuilt exactly as they were.

One of my dorm-mates was a young girl from Spain who had just broken up a long-term relationship, and she was having a pretty hard time. Her father had died about a year ago, and her lover had finally left because she wasn't able to control the constant grieving. I could feel sorry for both of them. We walked and talked for two days. She had a job in a winery and served as their tasting expert. She was a great one for lunch at the outdoor cafés. We are still friends.

Berlin, Germany

Berlin was the only city where there was a nice hostel just across the street from the rail station, and neither of them were shabby as in so many other towns. In fact, nothing in Berlin is shabby. New and old buildings mix pleasantly. The train station is quite trendy, with nice restaurants and shopping. I saw the hotel window balcony where Michael Jackson dangled his baby to the horror of all the reporters present. I stood on the spot where Hitler's bunker was, but a guide had to tell us that we were there because there is no marker of any sort. The bunker has been filled with cement because they do not want it ever to be turned into any sort of monument. I saw Berlin's monument to the holocaust victims. It was very moving. There is a yellow line painted all through Berlin to show where the wall between east and west used to be. I saw Checkpoint Charlie.

I rode a public bus, and on the way around town, I saw a Bauhaus museum. The Bauhaus School of Art and Design was founded by Walter Gropius. He was an architect and design genius. His works are still shockingly modern, beautiful, and utilitarian. Google him if you are interested. His works have had a lasting impact on the western world. Walter Gropius was a Jew. He had to flee Germany in the '40s, so he came to the Boston area in the USA. He designed and built a home near Concord, Massachusetts. It was declared a USA National Landmark in 2000. I have visited it several times since I once lived near there. When I saw the Bauhaus museum, I was very anxious to go. I spent a happy day there. The museum covered Walter Gropius's life in detail, but I found it interesting that it never mentioned that he lived his last years and died in America.

Hamburg, Germany

Hamburg is a nice enough town, I suppose. I didn't see much of it. So why did I go, you ask?

Well, it was like this.

Way back, my second week out, when I was traveling from London to Belfast, remember that? There was a ferry leg involved. Somewhere in Scotland when a change was being made, a cheerful little man who spoke hardly any English asked me for directions to the ferry. I helped him. He was very grateful, and he told me that he was from Hamburg and he was going to Belfast to visit the Titanic museum. Did I mention that he was very cheerful?

Remember my story about the two-night stand with David? Well, as David and I headed out for breakfast the first day, we heard someone shouting on the street in Belfast. We turned to look, and it was the cheerful little man from Hamburg. He ran up to us so excited. He shook David's hand, kissed me on both cheeks, chattered happily, and then went away. I thought, *Now that is too bad. Now he thinks David is the man I came here to meet, and that is not true.* I could never have a crush on David, but that cheerful little man from Hamburg is a different story.

I didn't want to tell you this because I was afraid you could never understand and reconcile it with the terrible open sore of a heartbreak that I was living through at the time. But I have decided that I have to trust you, my readers, to understand that I had a crush on the cheerful little man from Hamburg. It was a silly fantasy, I know, but I used it to help me through when the loneliness became too intense to bear. So all summer—no, not *all* summer, just sometimes—I thought, *When I get to Hamburg, I'll find that cheerful little man.* But how? I don't even have a name. I considered buying the front page of the newspaper and telling my story. How crazy! Even if it worked, he would probably be outraged and embarrassed and rightfully so. No. I knew I couldn't find him, and I might not even like him if I did. But still … I couldn't resist coming to Hamburg. I guess I thought maybe magic would happen, but of course it was never meant to be.

So there! That is why I came to Hamburg. There was a nice park not too far from my hostel, and I mostly just sat in the park. And thought. And cried a good bit. And resolved to move on.

Cologne, Germany

Cologne is a nice town. They are especially proud of their cathedral, and it was very nice, but they should clean it. Oh my! I'd better go home. Have you heard me be so caustic before?

In my hostel, I met two young American girls. I was immediately struck by how fit they both looked, then I learned that they had just graduated college and had come to Europe for a year to play professional volleyball! Every time they had a few days off from training, they went somewhere, and this time it was Cologne. I have forgotten where they were based. We spent a day together.

While in Cologne, I was told that I should take a day trip to Bonn, but I couldn't see the sense of that since I had time on my hands. I just booked a hostel for a couple of days and planned to go there next.

On my last afternoon at the hostel in Cologne, I saw a small black woman standing in the middle of a room and trembling. She was obviously suffering intense anxiety. The hostel manager whispered to me, "Joy, that woman wants to stay here, but she is afraid. Go and reassure her that we are safe."

I spoke to her, and she just dissolved with relief. Here is Ada's story.

Ada's husband died recently. After he died, his family took all his belongings, including his house, and ordered Ada and her eleven-year-old daughter to vacate. I was aghast! Ada would have had all kinds of protection where I live, but she said they were immigrants (I didn't ask about legality). They lived in tight-knit communities, and in their culture, this was all perfectly according to custom. In some cultures, women, especially unmarried ones, have no rights or protections. She seemed afraid to go to the police. Ada and her daughter had little money and nowhere to go. Someone had recommended that Ada come to this hostel, but she had never seen a place like this before and didn't know if it was safe for her daughter.

Ada had left her daughter sitting alone in a restaurant across the street while she came here to check this place out. I told her that hostels in general were very safe, and this is a good one. I also volunteered to go with her to get her daughter. When we got to the restaurant, the daughter was sitting stiff and big eyed, but she broke down and sobbed when she saw her mother. I sensed that she had been afraid that Ada was not coming back.

Ada explained that she had to get up early the next morning to get her daughter across town to school. I already had made plans to leave the next morning so we said goodbye. I must admit I was anxious to get away because I was afraid of Ada. Afraid in this sense: I am a rescuer by nature and felt myself becoming too attached, too responsible for her, and I knew I couldn't save her. It tugged at my heart to leave Ada there.

Bonn, Germany

Bonn is the birthplace of Beethoven, and they are very proud of him. It is a beautiful little city, and I kept busy and happy for a couple of days. I was working my way closer to Brussels since I have an especially dear friend there, and I was anxious to visit her. This was now late September, and the weather was turning cool again. Also I noticed that the hostel clientele was changing. Not many tourists now. Mostly it was young people who have come to this city (insert any city name) for university or some training and were just in this hostel for a few days until other accommodations are found or made ready.

The last day in Bonn, I began to feel ill for the first time in a long time. I usually do not have colds or flu or anything bad.

Liege, Belgium

I moved on to Liege, Belgium, but I must go back there someday because I missed it. I was sick. The only thing I saw (and it really made an impression) was the train station. I just barely dragged myself out of bed to find food once or twice a day.

For goodness' sake, look up Liège-Guillemins railway station in Wikipedia. It is unbelievable. It was designed by the same architect who did the World Trade Center in New York.

Brussels, Belgium

By the time I got to Brussels, I was fine again. Chipper as ever. I love Brussels. All the superlatives you can say about a city are extra true for Brussels. I think it is by far the most beautiful! I love to stand in that square, turn around and around, and just gape at those glittering buildings! Other cities are other things, but Brussels is spectacular!

By this time, I was looking at the calendar and planning carefully. I mentioned earlier that it is a mistake to have an end point that you must meet. I was looking at my flight schedule and also at the end of my EU rail pass. I wanted to make my last trip on that pass be the train going from Brussels to London via the tunnel under the English

Channel. After that, there will not be much left on my bucket list. Because of this careful scheduling, I had about fourteen days to spend in Brussels. That was easy. Nowhere better to spend it.

I have a very special friend in Brussels, and I knew she would give me full attention once I called her, and I felt like fourteen days was too much to lay on her, so I stayed five days before I called her and said, "I'll be there tomorrow." Some people say even little white lies are wrong, but I am just not sure how to get by without them.

After I called her, she took me to some wonderful spots that I would never have found without her. We went to the beach and ate our fill of seafood. We went to the botanical garden, to a nearby village, and to the Brussels archaeological dig. Sometimes we just hung out and watched TV. Friends are the best. Especially some friends. On the last day, she took me to board the express train to London. It was the only time all summer that I traveled first class.

Ainara and me in Dresden

The holocaust memorial in Berlin

Berlin is a wonderful mix of old and modern. These are government buildings

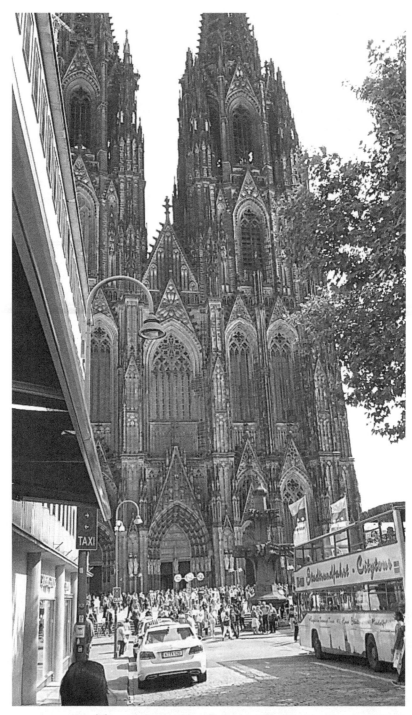

The cathedral in Cologne, Germany

Beethoven's birthplace in Bonn

The man himself

The Liège-Guillemins railway station, Liège, Belgium

Pictures cannot do justice to Brussels. That is gold on those buildings and it shines

Brussels the queen of cities

A very dear friend

CHAPTER 10

London Again

I stayed in London for another few days and remembered how much I like it. But it was October and getting cool again, and my sciatica was acting up. I'd best get back to my Arizona home for the winter. I booked a round-trip air ticket to Belfast with the return leg connecting in London to the flight I already had booked to Arizona. I picked up the bag I had left with my relatives and spent another week with my great family. Then I flew all the way home and stayed in my very own home for the first time in six months.

Home At Last

I started this trip for a reason and with a purpose in mind. Survival. Pure and simple. Did it work?

Well, yes, as well as it possibly could. The screaming sore I had when I started this is now a very sensitive scar. I can look at it much more objectively than I ever expected. But looking at it still hurts.

I don't expect that to get better. It will always hurt when I touch it, but I can live with that.

The effects of this adventure, other than that, have been phenomenal. Even at my age, I have grown and changed and learned so much. My shyness is still there sometimes, but not nearly as severe as before. If you find yourself in a queue with me, you can count on getting talked to. If you make it plain that I should be quiet, then I will, but reluctantly. I have learned that the world is so large and beautiful, and there are really people out there, and they are so nice. I am much more optimistic. If the world can just not destroy itself until that young generation that I met in hostels gets control, then everything will be fine.

But my biggest change is life-changing. Warning! This kind of travel is addictive. I'm going again next year to visit the special friends I have made and see the parts of Europe that I missed this year. I invite you to come along, but first I'd like to take you on a different kind of journey. See the next chapter for the story of another unlikely journey.

CHAPTER 11

Timeout from travel for a while. I think it would be a good idea if we get better acquainted. Let's just visit a bit.

People I meet sometimes say that they could never be brave enough to travel the way I do. They insist that some people are born with more courage and self-confidence than others. I don't think this is true; however, I do agree that some people are more fortunate in the nurturing they receive. Our parents are our primary nurturers, but other people we meet contribute to our self-image also. Characteristics, like muscles or habits, require practice to establish or grow strong. I shall tell you a story to prove that my self-confidence, although the seed was planted by my mother, took a long time to sprout and grow.

I was born to older parents. My mother was forty-two, and my father was in his mid-sixties when I was born. I had two brothers and one sister, aged nineteen through twenty-five when I got here. I was raised as an only child, of course. We lived on a farm in Oklahoma, and we were very poor. Our house was a shack, and I never experienced indoor plumbing, telephones, electricity, or locks until after I was an adult and left home. It was Depression days, and my parents said, "If anyone comes to our house hungry, when we are not at home, we want them to be able to get in." Things used to be like that in America. Long, long ago.

Life was so hard on that farm that my mother told my father that when her children were raised, she would leave the farm. There was tension in the home because my father was, as was not uncommon, cruel to his sons. No woman has ever loved a man who beat her babies. Mother was afraid to leave because she had no means of support, so how on earth could she take care of her children without the farm? Two months before my youngest brother would graduate from high school, I was born. My mother said, "OK, I'll stay here and raise this one … but don't you touch it!"

Given these circumstances, it would probably have been impossible for me not to grow up somewhat warped. I disliked my father but didn't really know why. I know now it was because I sensed that my mother disliked him, and I also knew that he couldn't touch me. I must have been a real brat.

So what did I learn from this period? I learned that men are impotent and not lovable or worthy, but women must have one. A woman is not complete and has no chance or place in the world unless paired with a man. I learned something else too. My mother and father never argued. I never heard either of them raise their voice. The lesson here is take whatever life gives you quietly.

In spite of being very poor, I had a happy childhood. A river ran through our farm for fishing and swimming. We had a big old barn with a hayloft to play in and on. My dad's passions were a fruit orchard, raising the best watermelons in the country and keeping a herd of small, spotted Welsh ponies. Put this all together and you can see why I was the most popular kid for miles around. I had a river to fish and swim, ponies to ride, trees to climb when the fruit was ripe, and watermelons on demand. Being poor didn't matter to a kid; everyone was poor. We ate and preserved what we grew, made our clothes from printed chicken feed bags, chopped our own wood for heat and cooking, and got by.

A typical summer day meant I would take ropes to the pasture and capture two or three ponies. I realize now that if they had not been willing to be captured, I never could have gotten them. I led them up to the barn, provided very basic bridles (we couldn't afford saddles), and rode one and led the others to my best friend's house. O.H. and Leon were also my cousins. O.H.'s name was Ormsby

Heinie III. So now you know why southern families often use initials. We rode the ponies, played cowboys and Indians, and visited every neighbor within five miles. Sometimes, instead of country roads, we explored the river bottom. It was mostly unfenced, boggy, wild lands. Sometimes we picked enough wild plums to take to the nearest village and sold them door-to-door for enough money for an ice cream each.

Much of Oklahoma is Indian land. On their land the Native Americans typically have a community house for meetings and pow-wows and such. My home was near enough to hear their drums and chants, so that was my go-to-sleep music on many summer nights. The Indians were our friends and neighbors. We were all acquainted and visited and played together often.

Once I overheard a neighbor lady ask my mother if she didn't worry about me when I was just gone all day like that. My mother replied, "If the good Lord didn't take care of them then, they wouldn't none of them grow up."

I am making a point that I alluded to above. It's about nurturing.

It is impossible to teach children not to be afraid. That can't be done. What can be done is to refrain from teaching them to be afraid. That is what my mother did. Natural, needed fears such as sudden movements or sounds, obvious dangers, predators, and such are taught to us by evolution. It is ideal if parents do not add to that list. I realize this is hard to do because you must first release all the fears that you have been taught. Worry is just another word for fear. It is the fear of imagined things that haven't happened yet. You must release that one too.

If your reply to this point is "I am not afraid, but I tell my children there are these things you must be careful of," you are telling them what to be afraid of. I think you should be careful not to teach your children to be overly fearful.

My mother never told me to be careful of anything. She told me I was a good girl, and I believed everything she said. When I was a teenager, I would go to school, but if some special extracurricular event came up (I played basketball and most other activities), I would just not catch the bus home, go to the event, and then go to my aunt's or cousin's house in town for the night. Remember, we had no telephone and no car. Mom had no way to know. She just trusted me, and I am happy to say I did not betray her trust.

I do remember this. I was about six when some distant relatives visited our house. One of the young men (eighteen-ish) started a game by which he hid a small article (a button maybe) on his person, and I was to find it. When my mother saw this game in action, she did not scold or explain, but she did put a stop to it. I never forgot that, but was much older when I understood why. I guess you can see that I would like this whole book to be a tribute to my wonderful mother.

I never took what my father told me quite as seriously as what my mother said. He did tell me one thing to be afraid of. This is kind of funny. Only one. At the time, it was a little confusing, and by the time I finally figured out that he was right, it was too late. My father's only directive was "Don't ever let a man touch you!" How different life would have been if I had followed that directive. It sounds very enticing in retrospect, but I am not really sorry for any of my life, just as it happened.

My mother was very involved with the community church. It was her only socially acceptable access to any social life. We had no car, so three times a week (twice on Sunday and Wednesday prayer meeting), Mom went to the lower pasture, caught the team of ponies, hooked them to a small wagon, and took me and the neighbor lady and her children six miles to church. This church was very conservative. Women and girls should not wear pants or any makeup or jewelry. Pride, you know, is a sin! Speaking of sin, I learned that lots of other things fit in that category too—movies, dancing, etc. Oh, yes, and divorce! Worst one of all! Put that with my training regarding men stated above, and you should be able to see my problems developing already.

Here is a bit of good news, though. My mother always told me that I was as smart as anyone in the world and I could do absolutely anything that I wanted to! And I believed her. Another thing that I learned from my mom was her positive attitude. Once, much later, I remarked to her, "Mom, you've had a pretty hard life, haven't you?" She replied, "Oh, I don't know. Life is about what you make of it!" I still think that was an astounding reply considering what I knew of how hard her life had been.

Nobody ever suggested that I go to college. The idea wasn't planted in my head. The high school I attended was small; there were only twelve students in my graduating class. It taught boys to be farmers and girls to be farm wives. Little else was imagined. After I finished high school, I moved to the nearest city, got a job (thank goodness I had learned typing), sowed my wild oats for a while, and was terribly homesick. I even went so far as to get an evening job selling candy at the concession stand in a movie theater. Now that is wild!

After a few weeks, I ventured into the city church that I knew my mother wanted me to attend. There I found what I wasn't expecting. The youth leader was a single, handsome young man who sang solos with a voice like an angel and all the girls in the church were after him. He had announced that his life plan was to be a missionary. I thought this was exactly what my mother would want for me, and my competitive juices kicked in. I looked no further; I married him!

Chapter 12

Really, girls, there is more to a man than his church affiliation. In fact, after I married him, he didn't go to church any more. Because of his status as a (mildly) wounded Korean War veteran, he could get a job at any government office upon request. Within two weeks, he would be telling me how they were mistreating him at work, and soon thereafter, he would quit. He was unemployed more than he was employed. Nevertheless, he never saw a dotted line he wouldn't sign. We were always one step ahead of bill collectors who were trying to take back his toys. He bought everything he wanted—cars, boats, outboard motors, fishing and camping gear, appliances, you name it. On one occasion, he decided to buy my mother a new refrigerator. It involved trading in her old one. Of course, he didn't make the payments, so the company came and got the new one, leaving Mother with nothing.

We bought a nice new mobile home but were soon in trouble because we couldn't pay the rent in a mobile home park. His parents owned some unimproved land just outside the city, so we moved our home out there. There was no plumbing, and electricity was via an extension cord, I don't remember from where. We hauled our own water and got by. He built an extra room onto the mobile home. I was pregnant, and he thought we needed the space. The room used concrete blocks for foundation. It was six by eight feet and leaned against the mobile home covering the back door. After a few months of this, the mortgage company came and took the mobile home away, leaving us with a six-by-eight, three-sided room on concrete blocks.

I nailed one of Mom's patchwork quilts on the third side so the rain would run down it instead of coming in. My kitchen (dishes, groceries, and a hot plate) was stored in boxes and washtubs, which were pushed under the floor of the room. Each day I would pull it all out and make meals. I saved the dirty dishes in a wash tub, and the next day, after the neighbors (about fifty yards away) had gone to work, I'd drag the tub over and wash the dishes using their outdoor faucet. Cold water of course. This was to conserve our own water, which we had to haul from his parents' house in town.

My husband acquired lumber and built a larger room to attach to the smaller one. All this happened, thankfully, before winter. We had a real house again, even if it had no insulation or foundation.

During this time, he was required to make an overnight trip because of the job he had at the moment. When he came home, he left his suitcase for me to unpack. While folding everything away, I came across something that initially bewildered me and then sickened me. His suit pants were covered with blood at the front. He had obviously kept his pants on for a quickie. I could not bear to touch them and immediately turned away.

I was so devastated that in the middle of the night, I walked to an oil drilling rig (there are plenty of those in Oklahoma), climbed to the very top, and tried to jump, but I didn't have the courage. I was saved perhaps because I had been taught that suicide, too, was a sin.

I believed that all my life would be changed because of that event. I thought everything I would experience from here on out would be labeled as 'before that event' or 'after that event.' That has definitely turned out to be completely untrue. To all you young ladies out there, when something horribly devastating or heartbreaking happens to you... don't jump off the rig. It will pass.

After seven years, we had two children and had moved to Phoenix, Arizona. I had a full-time job, of course. One day, a truck backed up to our house and took all our furniture and appliances. The men were assertive, and I didn't have the self-confidence to resist them.

My husband was not at home. Earlier he had asked permission to mortgage these things, but I had said no. He did it anyway, secretly, by forging my name.

I sought out a lawyer—still not for a divorce, but to see if I could get my things back. The legal advice I got then was that possession is nine points of the law. If I had not allowed my things to be taken, the mortgage company could never have taken them, but since they had them, there was no way for me to get my furniture back. But the lawyer, I would never say he talked me into it or even suggested it, but before I left, I began divorce proceedings.

It was tough. I felt so alone and worthless and like a total failure. I was sure that God hated me. It was such a trauma that I was sick a lot. I don't think I could have made it through those days if my mother hadn't come to stay and watch the kids while I worked. We were cooking on a hotplate and sleeping on the floor. All the things I had dreamed of for life now seemed impossible. Life was over, and I had failed!

The only thing I had going for me was a good job. I had learned to be a keypunch operator based on my training as a typist. I operated the machine that punched holes in the cards that served as input to early computers. Though a helpful skill of the time, that job does not exist anymore.

One day, my old car began to fail, and I decided to shop for a better one. So, I set out to go used car shopping with my mother and two kids with me. While browsing in one car lot, the salesman and I somehow got deep into talking about travel- a natural progression from cars, I suppose. After some more conversation, he said to me, "Sweetie (he called everybody that), let's you and me go to Alaska!" Remember, I felt alone, worthless, and as though my life was over. Worse yet, I was a woman without a man. I knew he was serious, and the excitement of a new venture was just too much to pass up. I said, "OK."

My religious training was still relevant in my life. The legitimacy of our relationship was important to me, so we agreed to go to California (my home was in Arizona at this time) to get married because there was no waiting period in California. So, I took the day off work, notified my friends and family, and off we went.

Things changed drastically when we got to California. Out of the blue, he told me that he had changed his mind, saying a wedding was not necessary and that he didn't want to do it. I was caught completely off-guard by this turn of events. Things had finally begun to look up, and I felt the familiar sting of disappointment all over again.

When we got back to Arizona, I was too embarrassed and humiliated to tell anyone. I let everyone believe we had indeed married. My church did not allow jewelry, so the lack of a ring was not an issue.

I was miserable.

I sold my house and car and quit my job. We went to Alaska. That was a marvelous adventure. We camped out every night on the way up. Once, we camped inside a heavy equipment barn. We pitched our tent and built a campfire to boil water and make dinner. When we went to bed, the fire still burned and the water still boiled. The next morning, the water was frozen solid. All this happened inside the barn. As we traveled, the kids were kept entertained watching for moose and were rewarded often. They would often shout, "I see pootfrints!"

We went in the early spring and came back in autumn. I thought we had gone to stay, but that never worked out anywhere, as I learned later. This man, who the world thought I was married to, seldom held regular jobs, never did anything illegal, yet we never wanted for money. He was a modern-day version of a horse trader. He just bought and sold things, and he was good at it. You may have heard of the salesman who was so good he could sell refrigerators to Eskimos? Well, he really did that. At least he didn't buy stuff on credit.

While in Anchorage, Alaska, he rented a furnished house with a good-sized, detached garage. He set up the garage with all the necessary equipment for a 'detail' shop and hired a helper. Then, he offered his services to every used car lot in Anchorage. They called us every time they got a trade-in. We would pick it up and return it 3 days later with the engine steam cleaned and painted, tires replaced, upholstery deep cleaned and dried, and every surface gleaming. The car would be ready for the front line at a much-improved price.

My job in this venture was to ferry the cars back and forth. In 4 months, he had a very profitable and well-established business. However, he was not the type to settle down and run it. He sold it at a price that seemed outrageous to me, and we headed back south.

He was always a traveler by nature- we never stayed anywhere, and we lived in every town up and down the west coast of America. We had a trailer hooked behind our car in which we would pack everything we owned: clothes, kitchen utensils, bedding, and all things personal. As we drove, he would, for mysterious reasons, pick out the new place he wanted to live in, saying, "This town looks promising. Let's try this one."

The first step was to find a furnished house to rent and move in. Then, he would go out and look around for an earning opportunity. Sometimes, our stay would be as short as a week, and other times, it lasted for several months. But every time, without fail, he would come in, and for an equally mysterious reason, say, "Sweetie, Let's leave this place!"

We would have everything we owned in the trailer tied down by bedtime. In the morning, we would shove in the remaining things at the last minute, tie the corner down and be on the road by daybreak. We never knew where we were going. We just drove until he had that mysterious feeling again, the one that would draw him to strange towns. I loved the feeling of driving through a town at daybreak, watching it wake up, the early delivery people running errands, realizing that I had everything I owned in the trailer right behind me, and maybe, just maybe, this would be home for a while.

One day, after he had been 'looking for an opportunity,' in Port Angeles, Washington, he came in and said, "Sweetie, I bought a fish boat." Now *that* was the beginning of an adventure. I set out to decorate that little boat like you wouldn't believe! I carpeted it, installed Formica, and set up window curtains. That boat quickly became the laughingstock of the fish wharf. My man (I still can't bear to call my husband) roamed around, talking to the other fishermen, quietly learning how to fish.

When the season opened, we set off energetically. Our boat was a salmon troller (not a trawler). That meant we used hooks rather than nets. He pulled in the fish with a hydraulic pulley while I cleaned them, throwing them in the hold and later going down and packing them with ice. During those days, I got so good that I could dress clean salmon at the rate of 3 a minute.

Of course, you must have the proper equipment to achieve that speed. We sometimes stayed out in the Pacific Ocean, near the 20-mile shelf, for 5 days at a time. Stays were limited by your ice and freshwater supplies. When the fish were biting and plentiful, it was fun, but when they were scarce, it was awful. Giant whales would often try to scrape the barnacles off their backs by rubbing on the bottom of our boat.

Overall, the whole fishing thing is a lot more fun to talk about than it was to do. We got by, but we made more money buying and selling boats than we did fishing. We lived and fished in several boats before that old urge forced us on down the road.

Honestly, I loved this nomadic life at first. It was different from anything I had ever known before. But after a while, I began to long for a home I could count on. I wanted to plant flowers and watch them grow. I wanted my children to attend a whole school term in one school. But when he said "go," I had no choice. I had no money, no job, no training, and no life prospects. Two children depended on me, and I felt the need to comply. But slowly and surely, I began to say "Why?" and "Where?" more often.

One day we left Eugene, Oregon, because he said we were going to Las Vegas. When we got there, he decided he didn't like the looks of the place and refused to stop. We hurried on to Los Angeles, but he didn't feel the need to stay there either. When he turned back north, my patience finally ran out.

"Stop at Bakersfield!" I exclaimed, "I'm going to unpack our things, and the kids and I are going back to Phoenix to stay with my mom. When you get really settled somewhere, you can send for us."

He was quite bewildered by this sudden outburst and stopped at Bakersfield, where we went into a diner. He bought a local paper and read the advertisements for jobs.

"There is a job advertised here for a used car manager in Coalinga (a nearby town)," he informed me, "If I can get that job and settle here, will you stay?"

Well, that was all I really wanted, so I said yes.

While we were in Coalinga, he came home with the news that his employer was having a Christmas party for the employees. He added that he would attend but couldn't take me along. According to him, I just simply didn't have the social graces to mingle with that level of people. He went to the party with the car salesmen, mechanics, and their families, while I stayed home and cried.

The self-confidence that my mother had planted had not yet begun to grow.

Let me add this, though. I knew he was wrong. I knew I was as good as those people. I knew that if they met me, they would like me. What hurt was that I thought he really believed what he said, and I was devastated that he thought so little of me. I had never been taught to argue. It just wasn't done. My frustration and hurt emerged through my tears.

When we left Coalinga (you knew we would), we went to Olympia, Washington- back near our fishing adventure. While in Olympia, something life-changing happened to me. I got a job! I had tried to apply for jobs before, but we were usually in towns so small they didn't have companies large enough to have IT (Information Technology) departments. But now, I was working as a keypunch operator again.

In Olympia, I found a house for sale. It was vast but very old. A couple had raised their family there. The wife had recently passed away, and her husband just wanted to take a few of his personal belongings and go live with his kids.

The price was reasonable, so I went to the credit union where I worked and asked if they would loan me the money. They refused because they didn't make real estate loans, but they did lend me enough for a down payment. With a newfound passion, I went back to the seller and negotiated some more. In the end, I got the price down enough so that what the credit union gave me as a down payment was really the full price.

When I bought that house, my 'husband' had a severe physical reaction. He knew that was the end. I now had a job and a home. It had been seven years.

CHAPTER 13

Before I knew it, it was time to move into my new home. However, the house was full of furniture and paraphernalia of the previous owners, so it all had to be cleared out before I could move in. Even the dresser drawers were full. I guess the old man's children didn't have the heart to clear their father's things out, so the responsibility fell on me. I cleared out all the extra clutter and actually ended up selling enough antiques out of that house to pay for it.

Then, it was time to refurbish the place. I remodeled the house myself and even re-wired, re-plumbed, and re-decorated. The kitchen did not look particularly appealing, so I installed a new kitchen as well. When I first got the house, I didn't have the practical skills to completely redo it. However, whenever I came across each problem and each change I wanted to make, I simply went to the home store and asked for help. The process was slow: I would go home with the supplies and instructions for that one task, and then I'd go back and do it again. However, the ability to ask for help and do things by myself meant that the seed of self-confidence was sprouting within me.

While undertaking the move, I decided to also attend adult evening education at the local high school. The course I chose was "Introduction to Computer Programming." It clearly stated that it would not teach you to be a programmer and would only determine whether you had the aptitude for it.

The first evening of class came, and the instructor gave us a test.

In the next class (we met weekly) he said, "There is someone in this class who, if they are not already a programmer, they certainly should be!"

To my utter shock that person was me! I was thrilled and completely ecstatic. I spent the rest of the class, the week even, doing nothing but daydreaming about being a programmer.

That same week, a position opened for a trainee programmer where I was currently working as a keypunch operator. I applied for it with great anticipation but was unfortunately told that they would never hire a woman as a programmer. They could do that back then.

Olympia, where I was located, is the state capital. Someone suggested that I get on the state's roster as a trainee programmer since all it required was passing a test and experience as a computer operator. So, I decided to go ahead with it. The test was the same one my instructor had given on my first day of class. I completed it faster this time and even better. The test was done, but the issue of experience was something else entirely. A keypunch operator is NOT the same as a computer operator. Well, if you haven't got experience, and it is something you must have, then what on earth do you do about it? That was what I did.

The committee was impressed with my test score and called my boss for a reference. He was quite puzzled and informed them that I was not a computer operator. (He might just have helped me if I had given him a heads up, but I hadn't). The state then called me in, took my name off their roster, and gave me a severe tongue lashing. I went home and cried and cried. Though I had tried not to get my hopes up too much, I was still optimistic about this job, and now it was taken away from me.

After this ordeal, I went back to my evening class. Yes, this was still going on. My instructor noticed my sullen face, so I told him my whole sad story.

"Now listen!" he said. "The state highway department has a separate hiring department from the rest of the state...AND the IT department director is a friend of mine. You go there, get on their roster, and give them my name instead of your boss' as a reference."

So, I went and did exactly that. When I was presented with the very same test I had been given two times before, I went ahead and aced that sucker!

Still, there was a problem. They called immediately and said, "We would like to hire you. The problem is we don't have an opening as a trainee programmer, but we want to hire you as a computer operator until such a position opens."

I had no experience as a computer operator, but I knew that this was my last shot. If I said no there would not be another chance.

So, I said, "I'll be there."

When I got there, I paid attention, tried hard, and learned to operate that computer before anyone could figure out that I didn't know how to. That was not quite as impressive as it sounds now- the computer was known in the industry then as "second generation." It was not nearly as complex as the ones that are in use today. In fact, it was just a glorified report writer - cards in, printed reports out.

The programming director gave me some books published by IBM, a self-study guide for COBOL programming. I took them home and studied, poring over the pages and absorbing as much as I could. Then, he gave me an assignment - a simple program to code and run, not on my computer, but on the new, 3rd generation, big boy over in the corner. I coded the program, keypunched it on my own time, and presented it to be tested on the big computer. I stood watching, and when the tape drive began to turn, and I knew it was because my program told it to, that was the most euphoric feeling of power and control that I could ever imagine having. The director was very impressed with my program and installed it into the system for everyday use.

A few weeks later, they hired a new trainee programmer. A few weeks later, another trainee joined the team. I was perplexed by this turn of events, so I went to the director and said, "I thought the first opening would be for me?"

He said, "No, Joy, you are not a trainee. I am going to give you the first full programmer opening!" And he did!

After it was known that I was moving into programming, one of the keypunch operators said to me, "Joy, you are so lucky!" I did not answer her smartly, but I was aware of the potential. My achievements didn't have much to do with luck.

During the next few years, I learned to solve problems and have confidence in my solutions. I bluffed a lot (and failed a lot), but I loved the profession intensely. I was ambitious, always did my best, and willing to work very hard. I took every class available to learn more. Eventually, I was promoted to more challenging jobs, becoming a systems programmer and then a systems analyst.

Much later (in 1979 to be precise), when I was conducting technical seminars for a consulting company, my company got a request for education from the Central Bank of Kuwait. My boss was aware that an American couple had recently been stoned by a Saudi Arabian mob because they caught the lady driving her inebriated husband home from a social evening. Thankfully, the police had got there in time to save the American couple. My boss said he would not allow his lady instructor to go to Arabia, citing the very same incident. However, I was determined. I went to the boss's office and pleaded with him to change his mind. Kuwait, after all, is not the same as Saudi Arabia.

That was my first time ever traveling outside of the USA, and I had to get a passport to be eligible for travel. My flight was rather long, and I changed planes in both London and Paris. The entire experience, after being in one place for so long, was absolutely surreal. As we neared Kuwait, the passengers began to go into the restrooms and come out dressed differently. Business suits changed to white dishdashas and Paris fashionistas emerged in black burkas. I was entranced but also scared silly.

When we de-planed (no jetway), I nervously quickened my pace because I thought I was in the exhaust of the jet engine. But, no, it was just a summer evening breeze in Kuwait. Also, there was an overwhelming odor due to which the other passengers were making loud noises of disapproval. However, I was from Oklahoma and recognized the smell of oil refineries. I just said, "Mmmm. Smells like money!"

The considerable time difference between The United States and Kuwait had completely befuddled my company administrator regarding which day I would arrive, and so there was no one at the Kuwaiti airport to meet me. Baggage was scoured because Americans were not trusted to not bring in excessive amounts of alcohol. After collecting my luggage, I was at a loss as to what to do next. A gentleman asked me where I wanted to go.

"I don't know," I whined.

So, he turned to a taxi driver and said, "Take her to the Sheraton." That sounded good to me.

At the hotel, I asked the taxi driver to wait while I went in to get local money to pay him.

"How much will one of these buy?" I asked the clerk, waving my dollars at her.

She replied, "It will take four of yours to buy one of ours."

I began to get a sense of the order of things. I found out that I did indeed have a reservation, but it was for tomorrow.

When the bellhop set my bag down in my room, he asked me something, but I did not understand. I tried to second guess what he was asking and answered him. He then spoke again and I guessed at answering him again.

At this, he let out a big sigh and said very clearly, "Oh, dear. You don't speak English, do you?"

I had never learned to adjust my ears to listen for an accent. Once I crossed that hurdle, we understood each other quite well.

I had been warned that taking pictures would be frowned upon, but I decided to go check out the town the next day.

I asked the hotel clerk for directions to anywhere, and she said, "Oh! You mustn't go outside."

That was a shock, but I tucked my camera out of sight and went out the back door anyway.

I was in a large dusty square with many strangely dressed, brown-skinned people. I assumed they were Kuwaitis. I was frightened but determined to see as much of this foreign land as I could. Quietly, I dashed behind a parked car, held my camera high over my head, and snapped a picture. Then I dashed over to the next car and did the same.

Soon, I noticed that the crowd had stopped talking and were watching me. I became alarmed and rushed back to the safety of my hotel. I later learned that the only church in Kuwait (Catholic) stood just across the square, and, it being Sunday, the Indian housemaids and drivers who wanted to attend mass had the afternoon off for that purpose. It all began to make much more sense. It turned out that the clerk told me not to go out because she didn't think I could stand the heat. I also learned that when English is your second language, meaning is often traded for brevity.

Later that day, my assigned caretaker from the bank found me, and I was given a briefing for my work in Kuwait. Classes began, and on the first day, in the middle of my lecture, the call to prayer burst forth from the mosque just across the street. That was rather unsettling, but I learned to take a short break so those so inclined could pray.

I had been contracted to teach every class my company offered on my specialty. That meant 6 weeks of teaching, but the courses were not designed to be conducted back to back, and there were many overlaps. After about 3 weeks I was drained. It felt as though I was repeating myself constantly, and even the student's eyes had begun to glaze over. You know it is too much if you have ever had to listen to more than 3 weeks of technical instruction. So, I went to management with a proposal: I'll stay my entire 6 weeks but let me stop teaching, let the students use what they have learned. I will help as their questions arise, and I could also help tune and debug the existing systems.

That worked out very well. If the Kuwaitis had sent a delegation to the West to hire, they would not have hired a woman. But I was already there, and they saw that I could help them. So, before my time was up, I was offered a very nice contract to design and develop a major new system for the bank.

I went back home, quit my job, packed my necessities, and moved back to Kuwait to stay.

My contract required that I design a custom system for the bank whereby their customers could hold accounts in any of the three major account types and in any of the world's seven major currencies. They also wanted to switch between them at will, using real-time exchange rates and other requirements that were unique to this bank. I was also to supervise the development and implementation of the system.

After my design had been approved by the bank, they sent a delegation to London to hire programmers to develop it. I didn't get to go (I was still a woman). Among the people they hired, there was an exceptionally brilliant young man from Belfast named John - I liked him a lot. We finished our project in Kuwait and then moved to America together.

After we moved to America, John became far more successful in his career than I ever did. He was dedicated, courageous, and absolutely brilliant. I stayed married to him for 37 years. I had finally found a keeper, and I *kept* him as long as I could.

CHAPTER 14

This year's adventure began differently than last year's, and yet, very much the same. I was determined to pick up where I left off last year and continue my exploration of eastern Europe. However, no trip to Europe can happen without a stop to see my beloved family in Northern Ireland.

Prague, Czech Republic

When I arrived in Prague, I went to the same hostel I had used last year and the receptionist remembered me. That made me feel so good and welcome. It was a good beginning for the rest of the trip. Exploring is fun, but the feeling of being in familiar surroundings is rather comforting sometimes too. I stayed a few days in the Prague I had come to love last year and then hurried on down to Český Krumlov.

Krumlov Again

If the name of this village confuses you, let me explain. Many countries in eastern Europe have towns and villages named Krumlov. This was no problem in the Middle Ages, but now, since they are all members of the European Union, you must specify which one you mean. Český Krumlov simply means it is the Krumlov that is in the

Czech Republic so locals tend to drop the Český when referring to their hometown. They know where they are.

This year brought an extra special surprise. Each year in June, Český Krumlov celebrates the Festival of the Five-Petalled Rose. The city is transported for three days back to the Renaissance period and the rule of the last Rožmberks. The streets and squares are filled with the roar of knightly jousting tournaments, historical crafts fairs, banquets, and medieval music. The highlight of the festival is a spectacular procession in historical costumes, featuring knights on horseback and particularly many notables linked to the history of the city. I did not know about this festival, but Zdenicka knew, and since my visit would coincide, she bought a full pass to all the activities for me.

It was beyond wonderful, but the best part was being with Zdenicka and Hana again. They make me feel so wanted and loved that it can cure any damage that may be done by the rest of the world. I spent days just sitting on their deck, watching the river fun, soaking up the love and feeling at home.

I stayed in Krumlov for two weeks and then cast off to see the parts of eastern Europe that I hadn't seen last year.

Festival of the five petaled rose

Festival of the five petaled rose

Old friends I guess

Festival of the five petaled rose

Festival of the five petaled rose

Festival of the five petaled rose

Festival of the five petaled rose

Festival of the five petaled rose

Festival of the five petaled rose

Festival of the five petaled rose

Festival of the five petaled rose

Festival of the five petaled rose

Festival of the five petaled rose

He has toy cannons that really work. Notice his toes. And his belt

Festival of the five petaled rose

Hawkers

Villagers

and their babe

CHAPTER 15

Bratislava, Slovakia

I took a Flix bus (a popular mode of transport in Europe) to Bratislava, Slovakia. I was now visiting places that I had not even heard of before! It felt amusing and exciting. What surprised me most about Bratislava was how the old town looked historic, stately, and lovely. I could soak in that atmosphere for weeks. In sharp contrast, my hostel was brand new and modern.

Over breakfast, I met a scientist from Brazil who was there to make a presentation at a science conference. Further discussion revealed that he was a regular user of an awe-inspiring computer program that I knew was used by scientists and engineers worldwide. When I told him that my husband had written that program, he was really impressed. We were both delighted to have met each other. It only goes to show that you may never know who you might encounter in the hostels.

I asked for advice about which other towns I should see in Slovakia and was told to go to Kosice (*ko see chee*). The recommended mode of travel was by train. The primary method of transport differed from country to country- in some places buses are better, but in other areas, the train service is better. This year I had not pre-purchased any passes, so I had my options open. The train ride from Bratislava to Kosice was one of the most entrancing I had experienced. I saw rolling hills, crumbling castles, lots of blooming flowers, mountains, and small villages through it all.

When I arrived in Kosice, I was tired and decided to take a taxi to my hostel. I showed the driver the address, and he nodded as though he knew exactly where to go... but he didn't. He circled and circled in little narrow streets. After some time, he stopped, and we got out and knocked on a door. It had no sign, but the name of my hostel was 'The Happy Bull.' The double doors were covered with a mural of a bull sitting on a barstool beside a naked woman. Well, this must be the place.

'The Happy Bull' was the strangest hostel I had seen so far. It was stranger inside than out- entry was into a hallway, and to the left was a dark bar. It gave the feeling of being covered in cobwebs, but I am not sure if it really was since it did not invite entry or inspection. Further back was yet another tiny dark bar where you stood to check-in. It was covered with dusty bottles in the background, and to the left of this were two small tables with a menu written on a blackboard on the wall.

After checking in, I was taken up a level to pass through a 'common room' which consisted of a larger table and two beds. If the dorms were full, I guess these beds were also given for rent, though they sure wouldn't have much privacy. Then it was time to head to my dorm. It was an attic room with 3 beds pushed into the slope so that if you sat up quickly, you would undoubtedly hit your head on the roof. On the other side of the room was one homemade bunk bed where the upper bunk was at least 7 feet above the lower bunk. There was a ladder, but I did not see anyone climb it. On the other wall was a homemade bookcase and on top stood the lower half of a naked department store mannequin. I was the first one there, so I chose the center bed.

After delivering me to the dorm, the gentleman who had checked me in disappeared, and it became eerily quiet. It was evident that I was alone here. I thought, "If my relatives could see this place, they would come and get me right now!"

As time went on, I was joined by two dorm mates. One was a young American Lady who was traveling in the opposite direction as me. She had just come from Romania (the place where I planned to go next), so I had a good time picking her brain about where to go and what to see. The other dorm mate was a young man from Bratislava. He came on the same train as I did, and his best friend had joined the clergy. The friend had gone through some training here in Kosichee, and the dorm mate had come from Bratislava to attend the friend's graduation ceremony. Neither mentioned finding this hostel weird, so I didn't mention it either.

After a lovely evening and a night's sleep, I decided this hostel was more 'colorful' than 'weird .' I gave it a rave review on my app. If you just relax and enjoy the strangest things, they can turn into your best memories.

The next day, in downtown Kosice, I was sitting in a park gazing at a beautiful old church when a lady rounded the corner and went inside through a side door.

I thought, "I'd like to see the inside! If she can do that, I can, too."

So I did. I had forgotten that it was a Sunday and instantly found myself inside a packed church. I was decked out in my tourist gear, and the service was going full tilt. I was too embarrassed since I felt I was interrupting them, so I sat down and tried to look like attending the service was exactly what I had meant to do. The music was excellent, and the service was in Slovakian, but it was just as moving as it is in English- maybe even more so.

After Slovakia, I wanted to visit Romania. My map said the best way was to begin in Cluj-Napoca, but there was no way to directly get there. The only way was to take the train through Budapest, which was quite the backtrack. It was too long a journey for one day, so I reserved a hostel near the Budapest train station for one night. When I got to Budapest, it was mid-afternoon. I had already been here last year and didn't really want to be a tourist again.

Moreover, I was exhausted and just wanted to rest. So, I found a hotel near my hostel, sat in their bar, drank beer, and ate peanuts until bedtime. It may seem odd to include this experience in a book where I am talking about my best memories, but I absolutely had to include that one. Somehow, it stands out and lingers still because I felt incredibly relaxed and at ease, and I love peanuts!

Romania

During my stay in Cluj-Napoca, I stayed at the Transylvania Hostel. I was beginning to hear words like 'Transylvania', 'Dracula,' and 'vampires' a lot. Cluj-Napoca is a lovely city, and I was especially struck by its opera house and botanic gardens. During my tours of the town, I also bought a pair of cool walking shoes. I would not call myself a shopper since I don't usually go looking for things, but sometimes I see some items in the shop windows that I just must have.

One day I was out walking in a public square when I saw an old lady sitting on a bench. For some reason, she captured my attention - she was watching me. Each time I looked back, she would still be watching. Then she stood up, revealing that she was tall, beautiful, and old. Finally, I stopped and turned toward her, and she began to smile. I couldn't help being drawn to her at that point, so I quickly hurried to her. When I got to her, I knew she was not going to understand my English, so there was nothing I could do but hug her. After the hug, I just walked away but kept glancing back. She watched me and grinned until I was well out of sight. I think that woman and I shared a lot of memories, but I just couldn't remember what they were.

My hostel was very comfortable and friendly. When I was ready to leave, however, I came to learn that traveling in Romania was going to be more of a challenge than I was accustomed to. There were no trains and very few buses, so advance planning was necessary. I wanted to go to Sibiu (*Sib-ee-oo*), but no buses were available to take me there. I bemoaned my problem to the receptionist, and she instructed me to "call ride share". It was not Uber; they had their own brand. I tried to install the app but could not make it work because a local phone number was required to register for it. Finally, the receptionist (who had seen my frustrations grow by the second) agreed to call a car for me on her account, saying I could pay her later. I appreciated that because she took a chance on me.

I dragged my bag down to the pick-up location, and within a few minutes, a mid-sized truck with a lone driver stopped and identified himself. He loaded me and my bag and began to drive. Shortly, he stopped at a gas station and picked up another man. The new man spoke no English while the driver spoke some phrases.

We drove several hours through the countryside, me between these two Romanian men. When I told some friends about this, they were aghast and offered their sympathy for how scary it must have been. Actually, it wasn't scary at all! We joked, even with the few words we understood. The two men stopped at a village, helped me in and out of the truck, pointed to the toilet, bought me coffee and rolls, reloaded me, and then we were back on our way. When we arrived in Sibiu, they asked for the address of my destination. When they found it, they stayed with me until they were sure I was in the right place and safe—yet another fond memory of my travels.

Sibiu was smaller than most of the cities I previously visited but was just as charming. It was a quaint, historic old town with lots of outdoor cafes. The hostel (which was above a bar) was small and rather cramped. While settling in, I spoke briefly to a young man from Prague. He was very friendly, but we didn't get well acquainted because I only stayed one day in Sibiu.

The next day I was happy to get a bus to Bosrov. I gave the address of my hostel in Bosrov to a taxi driver, and he took me to the old town square. There, he pointed vaguely across the courtyard and started explaining something, but, of course, I couldn't understand a word. He seemed to think the ride was over, so I paid him and struck off, looking for the hostel based on the address. It wasn't exactly smooth sailing, but I finally found it. As I was checking in, someone came into the room behind me. I looked around and was startled to see the friendly young man from Prague who I had met in Sibiu the day before!

What a happy coincidence. We introduced ourselves. His name was Ondre. He made delicious breakfasts for me in the shared kitchen every day. Through conversation, I found out that he travels a lot and he really had the breakfast bit figured out. We explored Basrov side by side, visited Dracula's castle, and had dinner together. We just understood each other and hit it off right away. We had similar interests and laughed at the same things. It was the kind of instant friendship you feel will last forever whether or not you ever see each other again. It surprised me to be making so many of these intimate friendships with such young people. Age really doesn't matter - I had to get old to discover that.

My next stop was Bucharest (which was nice), but I was slowly getting tired. Moreover, I was alone again and missing Ondre, so it wasn't quite so much fun. Bucharest has some catching up to do, so it may compare favorably with most other capitols, starting with the graffiti. Do you remember how in year one of my travels, after about 4 months, I began to get tired, jaded, and even critical of things that I would usually have liked? I still love traveling, but 4 months at a time is just about enough for me.

I watched a charming regatta in Bucharest but deciding what to do next turned into an issue here. I had managed to get far away from everywhere I wanted to be! Folks here urged me to go to their beach town, but I just couldn't develop any desire for that. I realized that I was going to have to fly to get anywhere. I tried for Plovdiv, Bulgaria, but just couldn't make it work, and so decided upon seeing it later. I finally settled on Ljubljana, Slovenia, which I was scolded for missing last year.

There are discount airlines in Europe that are really cheap, but you better not have more than a carry-on for luggage, and you had better learn to obey every rule, or they will sneak up on you with extra charges. For instance, you must check in online 24 hours in advance, or they will charge you for checking in!

Ljubljana, Slovenia

Upon arriving at the Ljubljana airport, I walked past a shuttle that charged 9 euros for a ride to mid-town. I don't know why I didn't get on it, instead choosing to get into a taxi without asking the price upfront. I knew better, but I just got careless. I now know that I must never ever do that! The cab had a meter, too, but it was no protection from the amount I was charged. I am too embarrassed to tell you how much I paid in the end. In retrospect, I realize that I could have fought it, but I was rattled and in too much of a hurry.

After I got over my anger and decided not to blame all of Slovenia, I really enjoyed Ljubljana. It had a beautiful old town and a huge daily market which I always really enjoy. Every day I would buy fresh fruit to take back to the hostel to savor - sometimes, I would buy enough to share.

I also took a day trip to Lake Bled, which was picturesque beyond description. It had a charming castle you could visit, but it was only worth staying one day- I wouldn't prefer going there to stay for longer. Bled has 4000 inhabitants and over 5000 hotel rooms. Surely that tells you something.

When it was time to leave Ljubljana, I realized that I wanted nothing more than to work my way back to Ceske Krumlov for another 2 weeks. On the way there I spent several days in Linz, Austria. That was a very nice city, and well worth visiting for a few days if you are in the area.

my hostel in Bratislava, Slovakia

Welcome to Bratislava

A statue

A statue

takes a break

The castle on the hill. Almost every town has one

The view from the castle

The train ride to Kosiche

A ruined castle

The train ride to Kosiche

The train ride to Kosiche

Sunflowers!   And now the sun is this way so we see their faces

The Happy Bull Hostel. The beds are upstairs. Picture it

The menu

The dinner

The common room

The decor

Cluj Napoka. The opera house

The botanical garden

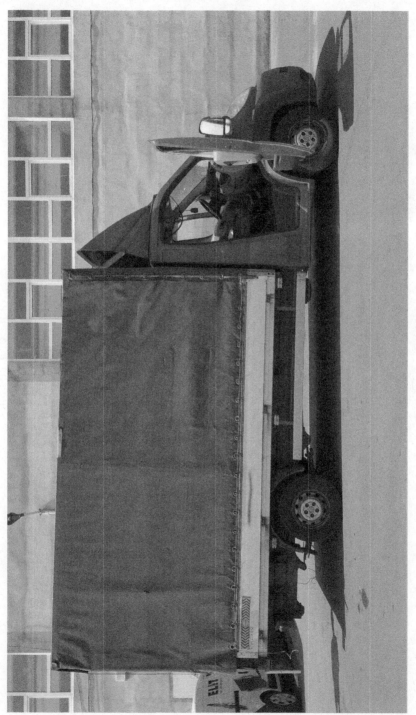

Ride share to Sibiu

Ride share to Sibiu

Sibiu

Brasov Romania. My hostel was hard to find

Brasov

Some houses in Romania have eyes

Bucharest

Also Bucharest

Guardians of the bridge into Ljubljana

Lake Bled

Linz is edging back towards the Alps

CHAPTER 16

Finally, I was back in Krumlov. Skippy and Hana knew almost everyone in Krumlov; therefore, I was slowly becoming acquainted with them as well. I got to know David, who owns a successful vegetarian restaurant. If I am in the mood to get kissed and be smothered with affection, I just go to see David. He says I remind him of his grandmother, and I am OK with that! I was also introduced to Zuzanna, who lives in Prague but operates a souvenir shop for tourists in Krumlov seasonally. I go there for good company and a hot cup of tea.

About halfway between Skippy Hostel and the downtown portion of Krumlov is a hill that requires a total of 80 stair steps to climb. There is a long way where you can go around the hill and avoid the stairs, but I love those stairs. I often climb them twice just to prove that this old lady can do it. Most importantly, it is to assure that this old lady will continue to do it.

One day, while out walking, I saw some lovely scarves displayed outside a small shop. I decided I wanted one but would put off buying it until tomorrow. So, I headed back the next day. They had a special, 3 for the price of 2, and, of course, I couldn't resist. However, right when I got to the counter, it began to rain. All the merchants were hurriedly starting to put out their umbrellas and raincoats. After I paid for my scarves, the merchant saw me about to head out in the downpour and said, "You can't go out like that!" Then he opened a plastic raincoat and put it on me. Now, every time I go back to

Krumlov, I buy something from that shop. The merchant and his wife have become my friends - that's the way it happens.

I did something last spring (before this trip started) that was very unusual for me. I agreed to purchase a guided tour of Spain and Portugal. It just seemed to me that it might be good to travel for a bit with people from my hometown. I stipulated no airfare and agreed to meet the tour in Spain. After two more wonderful weeks in Krumlov, it was finally time for me to start making my way toward Madrid to meet that tour.

I took a bus to Prague and then flew to Brussels. A very dear friend of mine, Mireille, lives in Brussels. I met Mireille about 10 years ago in Nepal. Since then, we have traveled and visited different places together often and are planning more. I love her and her husband, Ben, dearly. There are no hostels near Mireille's house, so I checked Airbnb and found a great one just a block away from Mireille's home. We didn't tourist much this year, mostly just *friended*. (New word. I'm surprised my spell checker took it).

After Brussels, I flew to Bordeaux to meet Ainara. You remember her? The Spanish friend I met in Dresden last year; she recently moved to Bordeaux. We met in a park using our smartphones for communication and directions. When we finally spotted each other across the park, it was such a special feeling - after a year of longing to meet again, *there she was*! We just flew into each other's arms, ecstatic to be with each other again.

Next, I decided to take a bus from Bordeaux to Barcelona. The Spanish tour I purchased only went to Barcelona as a 3-day extension, so I needed to see that city on my own. My bus was scheduled for 8 am, so I went to the station by 6:30 am just to be safe. The station was pretty empty when I reached, so I stashed my bags and went looking for coffee, but only found a vending machine. It took credit cards, but I couldn't make it work, probably because I couldn't read the instructions. I did have the correct change, though, so I tried again but to no avail.

Suddenly, a young man came along. He spoke no English, but he inserted and reinserted my coins multiple times, kicked the machine, led me to another, and proceeded to harass that machine until he finally got a cup of coffee for me. Then he asked if he could have a coffee. He looked like he could use one, so I said sure. I had no more change, so I produced a 10 euro bill. He tried to make this machine give change, but it wouldn't, so he instructed me to wait right here, claiming he would get change and be right back. (All this with no English). I was not surprised at all when he did not return. Oh, well! A small price to pay for a good story.

Soon, it became time for me to find an English speaker. When I did, I asked:

"Exactly where will I find my bus?"

They replied, "Not here! 20 minutes' walk!"

"But my ticket says this station!"

"Oh, but it doesn't mean this building. It means this general area."

NO! I had arrived an hour and a half early and was still going to miss my bus? No way I was letting that happen. I grabbed my bags and hurried out to the taxi stand, but nobody was there. So, I turned and headed in the direction the man had pointed as fast as I could. There, I was overtaken by a young lady.

"Do you speak English?" I asked

She nodded. "Yes."

"Do you know where the Flix bus station is?"

"I am going there."

"I have a bus in 10 minutes, and I am told it is a 20-minute walk!" I moaned.

She grabbed my suitcase in one hand and my arm in the other and upped the pace considerably, all the while chanting: "Don't worry! It's OK! We are going to make it!"

And we did! She put me on the bus and waved goodbye. All this happened between 6 and 8 am August 12, 2018.

Barcelona, Spain

Man, oh, man! It was a good choice to come to Barcelona. I had heard good things, but it truly exceeded all expectations! Barcelona is a city of marvelous buildings, wide boulevards, magnificent museums, and friendly people. Also, I must have hit the right schedule for street parties because they were everywhere.

If you ever come to Barcelona and are fortunate enough to meet Angela (a receptionist at my hostel), she may take you to a street party in her neighborhood. Each community has a team of castelleros, fully uniformed. They train, compete, and are judged on a point system similar to gymnasts. They must construct and deconstruct a human castle perfectly, all according to very strict rules and standards. The one on top is usually 4 to 6 years old. The blue team made a slight mistake and had to come down unsuccessful, but the brown squad had a good score, and the crowd was jubilant. I could never have imagined anything like that and would never have seen it except for the wonderful friendly people.

Barcelona is worth well more than a week for lovers of architecture, history, or just a good time. All the Gaudi buildings are amazing, especially the Sagrada Familia. It is not an ancient church like most, and is still under construction. It is financed with donations, so construction continues (still according to Gaudi's plans) as money becomes available.

My hostel there was nice, almost like a hotel, except I had roommates, which was the best part. I met a young man from Germany who made his living carving wooden watches. I could never have imagined such a thing!

Madrid, Spain

From Barcelona, I moved onward to Madrid. Madrid is also full of magnificent buildings, wide boulevards, magnificent museums, and friendly people. I planned to meet my tour here, but they only allowed 2 days for this great city. I am sure it was worth more than that.

I found a hostel in the northern part of town for one week and then moved to the southern part for another week. I really believe that the way I travel is by far the best way to do it. The cities, culture, street markets, and people are amazing, but the very best parts are the hostels. In Madrid, the atmosphere was delightful. Both weeks were like being with a caring, fun-loving family. I went out sightseeing every day. The hostels always furnish maps and instructions and provide guided tours. Each day I am bombarded with remarkable buildings, homes, monuments, and museums. And the shopping - oh, the shopping! Beautiful clothing from street vendors is so inexpensive that I can afford to do minimal laundry. I simply replace.

After I joined the guided tour, I enjoyed the rest of Spain. Valencia, Toledo, Malaga, and Torremolinos. Cordoba especially impressed me. The sights were so dazzling that I felt as though I had to be pulled away to stop admiring the places. The Islamic Mosque there was so large that when the Christians conquered the area, they did not destroy it; they just built a full sized cathedral inside it with plenty of room left over. You really can't imagine the beauty and splendor of this place without seeing it. Also, the Alhambra is magnificent and holds historic significance but the story that goes with it is heart-wrenching.

We also visited a farm that produced fighting bulls. Did you know those bulls have never seen a man not on horseback before they enter the ring? Buying the tour was certainly not a mistake. If you can only come to Europe once, this is undoubtedly the tour and country to choose. The tour finished in Lisbon, Portugal, in late September.

I stayed another week in Lisbon, and then moved on to Porto, a breathtakingly beautiful town. After Porto, I arranged flights back home to Phoenix, Arizona.

My new raincoat with a new scarf peeking out

Now and Then

IT'S GOOD TO PAUSE
IN OUR PURSUIT OF
HAPPINESS

just be happy

Guillaume Apollinaire

A sign on Skippys deck

Barcelona. A city of marvelous buildings

Barcelona. A city of marvelous buildings

Barcelona. A city of marvelous buildings

Barcelona. A city of marvelous buildings

La Sagrada Familia

detail

Barcelona. A city of friendly people. Angela

Madrid

Madrid

Madrid

Breakfast in the hostel

New shoes

New shoes

Me and Don Quixote

I'm being serenaded

Ronda

Ronda

Cordoba. This place really impressed me

Columbus's tomb

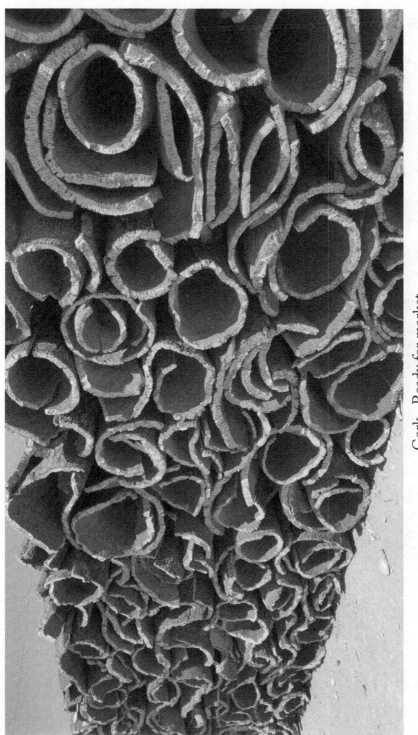

Cork. Ready for market

Porto

Porto

CHAPTER 17

Third Year
April 4, 2019

A few years ago, I traveled to Vietnam with a small group. That experience was so breath taking that I vowed to go back and bring my family from Belfast with me. Whenever I witness anything so excellent, all I can think of is to show it to the ones I love. So I had persuaded them to meet me in Hanoi. My plan was to stay on after they returned to their home in Northern Ireland and explore Southeast Asia on my own using the same travel style I developed in my last two years in Europe. The plan seemed rather smooth and exciting but unfortunately didn't work out that way.

One of the relatives coming was still in secondary school which required that we make plans around his spring break. I was unprepared for the difference in weather that the new schedule would mean. We had a good time anyway, but Lord!! It was *hot*! After my family left, I tried to stay true to my plan, but I just couldn't do it. I decided that I had absolutely no reason to punish myself like this and decided to come back to SE Asia at a more comfortable time of year. I got on the internet with the plea, "Give me the first reasonably priced ticket to *anywhere* in eastern Europe." I landed in Warsaw, Poland.

I loved Warsaw! The old town was enchanting and the new town was ultramodern. The history and culture of the area is captivating, the shops are good, and the people were friendly and kind—what's not to love? The only problem I had now was that Vietnam was too hot and now Warsaw was too cold, and I had absolutely no warm clothes. So, as I had done in London two years earlier, I found a thrift store and bought a temporary wardrobe.

I needed help to locate the thrift store, but by now, I was really good at asking for help. One of the employees at the hostel, Truda, volunteered to help me. As we became acquainted, Truda revealed an interesting part of her life.

Truda's Story

Way back in time, when the USSR still dominated Poland, Cuban youth were welcomed in the communist bloc to further their education. A young Cuban student came to Poland and had a fling with a married lady. The husband said they could keep the baby if it was white. It wasn't, so that family turned their back. The Cuban student stepped up and said, "I want it!" so the baby girl went home to Cuba with her father.

Fast forward six years, the mother and her racist husband have broken up, and the mother decided she wanted her baby back. Courts everywhere in those days favored the mother, so she won her case and went to Cuba to get her daughter. Truda told me that one of her earliest memories was screaming and clinging to her father's leg while the police tore her away.

Try to imagine her homecoming to Poland. She was six years old, did not understand the culture, and did not speak the language; her mother was a stranger, she had no friends, she missed her Dad, she was biracial in a white country, and it was time to start school. This kind of trauma would be hard on anyone but for a young child it is unthinkable.

Fast forward another seven years. At thirteen years, Truda will be legally able to decide where she wants to live, and her father was waiting in Cuba with open arms. Truda had adjusted to Poland, learned the language, made friends, and all her advisers were recommending that she stay in Poland. They said life was better here than in Cuba. So she stayed.

Many years later, Truda visited Los Angeles, California. Her plan was to hop down to Cuba and pay her father a surprise visit while in the USA, but she didn't understand the politics. Her return ticket was from LA. And she learned that if she went to Cuba, she could not return to the USA. Truda called her father to apologize for the near miss. Her father confessed that he was glad it hadn't worked out. It seemed he had a Cuban wife and grown daughters who did not know Truda existed, and he was afraid they would not take it well.

Truda cried when she told me, "At that moment, I realized I would never see my father again."

It seems like that story has ample heartbreak to go around. Think of both the father and daughter when they were torn apart, the daughter's experience in her homeland, the father's anguish when she chose not to return, and finally, Truda's dismay when she learned that she would never be welcome to see her father again.

The only happy part to this story is the ending. Truda is healthy, has a beautiful family, and a happy life.

While in Warsaw, I saw an advertisement on the internet for a last-minute deal on a cruise going from Copenhagen all the way up the western coast of Norway. I have been on cruises before, and I don't enjoy them - that is just not my style of travel. But, I really did want to see the Norwegian fjords, and it seemed to me that a boat was the best way to do that. I had time to spare, and the cruise fit right into my schedule, so I bought passage and started traveling west to meet the cruise in Copenhagen.

My next stop was Gdansk in western Poland. Gdansk had everything going for it that Warsaw did; it was only smaller. I really adored it. The Slowgate hostel there was the type that yielded lasting friends. Gdansk also had a WWII Museum that was perhaps the best organized and presented museum I had ever seen. For me, it was something that changed my perspective forever. I suppose all Polish people know their history, but I had never been taught what really happened to Poland in WWII. The very first shots of WWII were fired in Gdansk.

In the second week of May, Gdansk was still cold. I was grateful for my thrifty coat!

One day, as I was warming up in a coffee shop, an old man who was also a customer spoke to me. Well, he was not as old as I am, but he was old nonetheless. I answered his questions politely, and he moved over in the seat beside me and kept talking. I was not alarmed by this because people in eastern Europe (and Asia) are frequently excited to speak to westerners, especially Americans, for several reasons. First, I think they just want to practice their English, but I sense something underlying too. They want to be recognized by an American. They want to tell me how much they admire America. They want me to know that they are there, real people, and trying so hard to get it right! They are proud and happy that they are not communists anymore, and they want us to be proud of them too. They are so excited about the small things that we take for granted.

Anyway, back to the man in the coffee shop. He was from Gdansk but had emigrated to Dublin many years ago for a job. He had a degree in horticulture and was the groundskeeper for a resort in Dublin. He talked (as old people do) about Gdansk before the war, back in the 'old days. We spent the day together and agreed to meet again tomorrow, the next day, and the next. Though I was not grieving anymore, I was still terribly lonely most of the time. I had met many new friends on my travels that brightened great stretches of my time, but this man (his name was Robert) was different. We both knew that he would fly back to Dublin on Friday, and I would take a train to Malmo, Sweden. While we exchanged our goodbyes, he gave me souvenirs from Gdansk and his Dublin home and pleaded with me to visit him there soon.

Malmo, Sweden is a beautiful, friendly, and welcoming city, but I did not get the sense of history and culture there that I did in Poland. One thing that surprised me in Malmo was that cafes will not accept cash, even for a cup of coffee. You must pay for everything by credit card. They said it had something to do with an anti-money-laundering campaign.

I keep telling you all these stories about me bouncing all over the place, an old lady traveling incessantly, and I really hesitate to tell you any of the underside, the problems of my travel. They are the same problems that come with just getting old in general. One of the biggest issues was my sciatica, which I may have mentioned before. The pain can be extreme when I travel.

I heard some whispers over a year ago that CBD oil might help my pain. When I got home last year, I found a dispensary and bought some oil. They gave me directions for how to use it, but here is the thing: it wasn't cheap, and when I am at home, I don't have enough pain to justify using it. I am not sure what it is about traveling that triggers the pain, but it really does. So, all winter at home, I had the CBD oil, but I didn't use it.

When I flew to Hanoi in April, the pain was back after a day. I dug out my CBD oil and took what I thought they told me to. It did not help at all, so I took more and more. So much for CBD oil. It didn't work, so I bought a huge supply of pain pills and carried on.

Now that I was in Malmo, I decided to devote all the time here to myself. I went to a pain clinic, a Chiropractic Clinic, and a massage parlor. I got a pedicure, manicure, and a foot and leg massage. I got professional advice about which pain pills I should be using. When you are alone, you can't wait for someone else to pay attention to you, but you must do it yourself! The pain was still there, but I felt better anyway.

When I left Malmo, I took a train to Copenhagen harbor and went directly to my cruise ship. Wow, was I surprised! I mean, big is big, but this was outrageous! My cut-rate passage bought me the lowest level with no porthole. No problem really, because I didn't stay there much. Those Norwegian fjords did not disappoint - they were just breathtaking! I loved Iceland and Scotland also, but I remembered why I did not enjoy cruises. Well, to each his own.

After the cruise, I stayed a few days in Copenhagen. I think it is the most underrated of all European cities. It is full of fascinating tourist spots. The second oldest amusement park in the world is right in the middle of town. The oldest is in a nearby village. There were many attractions pointed out to me that I would have liked to have explored further, but I didn't. I'm not sure why I refused to, except for the fact that I was lonely. I missed Robert. If you would like to see Copenhagen, contact me since I'd love to go again. But be warned, it is very expensive so you must come prepared. I left all my temporary winter wardrobe in Copenhagen. Summer had arrived, and I decided to travel light from here on.

I flew to Prague and returned to my familiar hostel, The Mosaic House. From there, I called my friends Skippy and Hana in Krumlov. I was really anxious to see them, but I didn't tell them I was in Prague. I knew that the timing right now was too close, and I should have contacted them sooner. I was afraid that they would feel guilty if they had no room because I was in Prague already, and that was exactly the case. Skippy said that their hostel was fully booked for the next month because they hadn't heard and didn't know an exact date. She was so sorry! I said, "No worries. Just save me 2 weeks for the next available date." She gave me a date then, but it was a month away.

While in Prague, I called Ondre, the man I met last year in Romania. We had a long lunch and remembered that we enjoyed each other's company as much as before. I have decided that I love Ondre, and I must see him at least once a year or perish. This in spite of his being less than half my age. What a wonderful predicament!

Now came the question of what to do in the next month. I studied my map and realized that there was a major portion of Europe that I had not seen and wanted to see lying north of me. I decided to fly to Helsinki for a taste of Finland. I planned to take the ferry back across the Bay of Finland to Tallin, Estonia, and then a bus south through the Baltic States (Estonia, Latvia, Lithuania).

At a seaside resort in Latvia, I came upon a very strange hostel. Its atmosphere could best be described as that of an 18th-century mental hospital. There were long spooky hallways with echoes and big rooms with 10 or 12 single beds (not bunk beds as most hostels have). All my roommates were older ladies. I was used to all my roommates being quite young and chattering in English. This experience was strange - the ladies didn't talk, and one was making lace with a tatting shuttle. I decided to force some conversation along, so I walked up to her and admired the lace. She seemed delighted. The next day as she was leaving, she came by my bed and gave me the lace. She said "for your kitchen" in very halting English. I was really touched - that lace was weeks of work! I don't know what exactly to do with the lace, but I will treasure it always.

After my stint in Latvia, I moved on to Vilnius, Lithuania, and stayed a week. I liked it so much that I put it on my list of cities to visit again. This week, though, I did not find anyone to ask where to go next, so I studied Google Maps. Through the app, I decided I wanted to go to Minsk, Belarus. It looked like the logical next step, and the pictures online were enticing. From there, I could drop down into Ukraine and maybe even Moldova. Also, I would be near Chernobyl and could perhaps make a day trip (if that was even allowed!)

Next, I opened Airbnb and booked a room in Minsk. I knew the bus service was very good in this region, the buses were seldom full and ran often. Earlier, I had just shown up on travel day and said, "Give me a ticket on the next bus to X." On this particular day, though, it didn't work.

When I asked for a ticket to Minsk, the lady said, "So... do you have a visa?"

"What? Of course not!" I replied. "I've never needed a visa for anywhere I've traveled!"

"Well, you have to have a visa to go to Belarus," the lady said, crinkling her nose.

"Really? Well, how do I get one?"

"Call your embassy."

"How long do you think it will take?" I asked urgently.

"About 5 business days," she replied matter-of-factly.

"My room is booked for tonight! And I have given up my room here!"

"Sorry, here is the telephone number for your embassy."

"Thank you," I sighed.

I slunk away into a corner and called the embassy. The recording said, "This office is currently not available." Then I suddenly realized that today was the 4ᵗʰ of July. American Independence day! Heavens, they may not be back for a week! I decided right there that going to Belarus was too much trouble. Never mind the room deposit; that was minimal. But what to do? I had no plan B, and the day was wearing on. Sometimes, when you travel spontaneously, a glitch happens, and you just have to recover.

I studied Google maps and decided to go back to Warsaw. It was quite a long journey, and I had missed the earlier buses, but nothing in between grabbed my attention. I knew and liked Poland and Warsaw. I had already spent one week there this year, but another would be most welcome.

Regarding the aborted trip to Belarus, I have since learned that the Visa requirements are different when you travel by bus than if you fly. You can get a visa in the airport when you arrive, but if traveling by bus, you must get the visa at journey origin.

Gdansk, Poland

Gdansk, Poland

The ship

Some fjords

More fjords. From the ship

More fjords. From the ship

Fjords

Akureyri, Iceland

Tallin Estonia

my hostel in Parnu, Estonia

yet more doors to get in

In at last. Up more stairs

Long echoing hallways

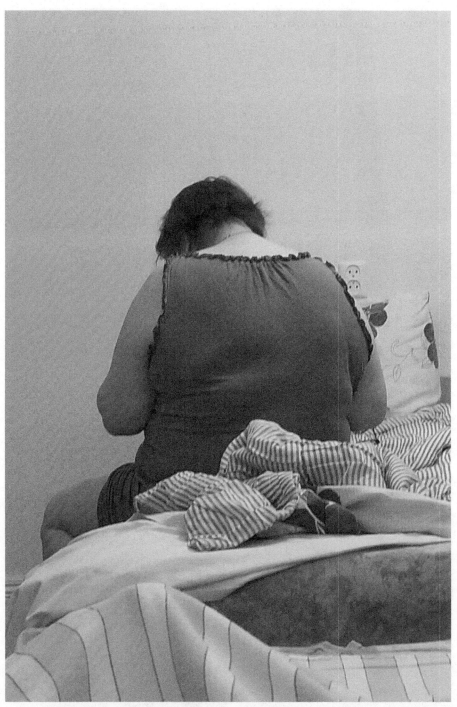

The lace maker

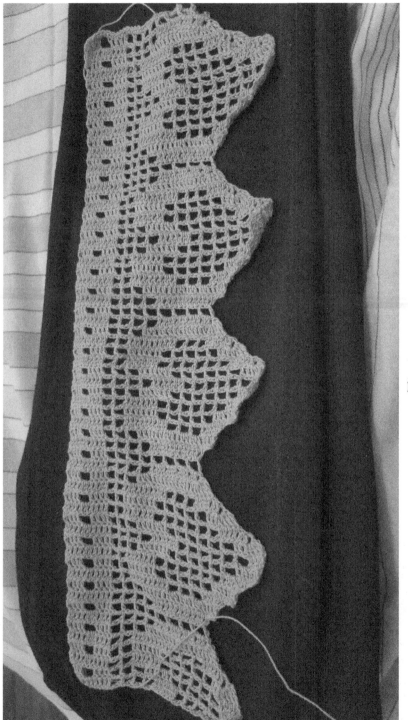

The lace

Vilnius, Lithuania. A fellow traveler

Vilnius, Lithuania.

CHAPTER 18

Here I was in Warsaw again! I liked Warsaw even better the second time.

On this visit, I got a different hostel in a much more central location. When my first day there commenced, I went looking for a hairdresser but instead found a cannabis shop! I decided to go in and discuss my total failure with CBD oil with them - perhaps they could recommend something better to help the pain.

The salespeople were very kind and explained in detail how it had to be used. They explained that this was not an 'on demand' pain killer. You must use a consistent amount for about 2 weeks before noticing a difference. So, I bought a new bottle, determined to do it right this time.

Voila! After 2 weeks, I could indeed tell the difference. My discomfort was so much better that just one painkiller a day would tide me over. That was a much-needed downgrade from pills far too many to admit taking.

I started out on a walk one day, deciding I would go sightseeing on foot. After about an hour, I realized that I needed my pain pill. Oh, yes, I had them. I never left home without them... except, I had forgotten to bring a bottle of water so I couldn't drink them down.

I decided to stop at the next sidewalk cafe, order a drink, take my medicine, and rest while the pill took effect. When I scanned the menu, I discovered that beer was less expensive than water, so I pointed at that. The waitress said, "If you have that beer, I will bring you two."

"No, no," I replied. "I only want one."

"You must have two because we have *permission!*" she insisted.

Well, I didn't know how to argue with that.

Sometime later, a young man brought my two beers, so I decided to try it again.

"Why must I have two beers?" I questioned.

"It is because we have a *promotion!*" the man exclaimed.

"Aha." I nodded.

But wait... there is more to this story! Beside each beer, there was a small square of something. I couldn't tell what it was without digging out my reading glasses.

Surely not sugar cubes...with beer? I dug out my glasses to solve this mystery.

You would never have guessed! It was bubblegum!

I enjoyed my two beers, took my pill, and rested a while even though it was not yet noon. Then I floated happily down the street, blowing bubbles like a kid.

Something else, far more important, also happened in Warsaw. I had heard about "Angloville" previously from hostel mates. I was interested and even made notes about it, but then I also promptly forgot about it. But in this hostel's common room, there was a large placard advertising "Angloville", so I called them.

Angloville is a company selling services in many countries but mainly in eastern Europe. Their target customer is anyone who speaks English but needs more practice to improve. They offer their customers a week in a resort with a native English speaker. They screen their 'native English speaker' volunteers carefully. What the volunteers get out of it is an all-inclusive week at a resort and a chance to get acquainted with locals.

It sounded perfect for me. A whole week telling stories and meeting new people! But when I called them, it was a bit too late to apply for this year. They had an opening available for one week in late August in... you guessed it! Warsaw! So, I will be back here for a third time this summer.

I had spent a month, and now it was time for me to go to Ceske Krumlov to visit Skippy and Hana. It was also time for an update on the CBD oil - it had been 3+ weeks, and I had no pain! None! Zilch! I didn't have to take pain pills anymore. If any of you are living with chronic pain, I recommend that you consider giving CBD oil a try.

Krumlov

Arriving in Ceske Krumlov was no longer a matter of figuring out how to get me and my bag to the hostel. I was met at the station by smiling friends and hugs all around.

I described the view from their deck way back in 2017 (my first year of travel). It was a delightful river usually full of rafters in the summer. There was also a rapid to be traversed just below Skippy's deck, which many didn't make without a dousing. This year, one of the other hostel guests wanted to go rafting but couldn't find a mate, so I volunteered to go with her.

My sweet friend, Hana, was very concerned for my safety. She scolded everyone she could find, trying to get someone to stop me, but nobody knew how to do that, so off we went. It was glorious fun! We surprisingly got through the rapids upright and so didn't even have to recover from a dunking.

Summer evenings are a delight in Krumlov, often spent sitting outside in that fairyland with a castle towering above and listening to Skippy, Hana, and Peter make music. It is magic - the crowds gather and dance.

One day Skippy took me to visit one of her friends named Vera. This involved climbing one of the steep mountains that surrounded Krumlov. On the very top was a chapel originally built as a monastery, which had long ago fallen into disrepair. Vera had found it and asked for permission to restore it. After the permission was granted, it was transformed into a delightful place for respite and rest. Vera and one helper were always there to greet hikers who found this place by chance. It was not advertised nor visited by groups. It was a jewel in the rough. I went back each day to visit Vera - she is a year older than I am, and it was hard to find others like her. We promised to meet again next year.

After long enough in Krumlov (I really didn't want to wear out my welcome!), I started going back North because I had an appointment in Warsaw with Angloville. I had been anticipating my week with Angloville ever since I had made the arrangement. I was beyond excited and expected many good things.

Google Maps suggested a town in Poland named Wroclaw as an interesting halfway point.

While in Wroclaw (pronounced 'wrote suave'), I realized my CBD oil supply was about to run out. So, I located a dispensary on Google Maps and set out to search for it, but could not find it. I knew it was nearby but couldn't see it. I also couldn't refine my search because I had no data and was not on Wi-Fi. I saw a large bank and walked into it, asking the receptionist if I could give her my destination shop name, and she could print out the information I needed.

She looked it up on her computer and said to her co-worker, "I'll be right back. Cover for me." Then she said, "Follow me". I thought she would simply point in the right direction, but she walked with me about 4 blocks to the dispensary and then stayed to act as an interpreter since the clerk spoke no English.

I walked with her back to the bank.

On the way, she asked me if I liked Poland.

"Very much!" I replied.

She seemed surprised. "Why?" she asked.

I replied that it was primarily because the people were so friendly.

She was even more surprised at this and said, "I don't think the people are very friendly."

I said, "Consider what you just did for me!"

One more thing before I conclude this incident. You may ask how is it that I knew, even before I spoke to her, that the receptionist spoke

English? And conversely, that the shopkeeper probably did not? It is a matter of age and education, both of which can be well judged at first sight. Anyone who is young and educated speaks English. If they are either older or less educated (you can guess at that by the job in which they are employed), they probably do not. This applies almost everywhere. However, in Western Europe, you often find people reluctant to speak English even when they can. In eastern Europe and Asia, anyone who can speak English is eager to speak it every chance they get.

So, I moved on to Warsaw for the third time this summer. I went back to my favorite hostel Centrum. The things I liked best about this one were its location (easy walking from the central bus and train station and central to attractions, restaurants, and shopping) and the fact that it was new, spotlessly clean and had great showers.

There was plenty to see in Warsaw, even on my third visit. I visited the 'Uprising Museum' which documented a particular era of Warsaw's resistance to Nazi Germany in WWII. It was very informative and moving. Before the uprising, the Polish knew they would lose, were outnumbered, outgunned, had no source of reinforcement or resupply, but decided to fight anyway. They held out so long that they made the Nazis absolutely enraged. When all the resisters were finally wiped out, the Nazis proceeded to methodically destroy every building miraculously still standing in Warsaw. There was a 3-D model of Warsaw at the end, in which there was not one building with a roof. It makes it even more amazing to see what a beautiful city Warsaw is today.

Another really special thing about Warsaw is its library, with an art gallery inside and a botanical garden on the roof. It is spectacular inside and out and well worth most of the day.

When the time finally came to kickstart Angloville week, the English-speaking volunteers met in the old town for a day of sightseeing, a nice lunch, and to meet each other. They were from the USA, UK, Canada, New Zealand, Ireland, Scotland... in short - all the English-speaking world! They were a great crew, very compatible, and fun. The next day we, and the Polish participants, all met in a large parking lot where a small fleet of buses took us about 50 miles out in the countryside to a resort in a small village. It was historic and beautiful.

The week that followed was so rewarding and so fun that it qualifies as one of the best memories of my life. We spent a week of comradeship, fun, games, learning, and great food. Angloville had everything so well planned and organized that there was never a dull moment. Lots of hilarious games interspersed with serious moments and chances to just get acquainted - planned learning at its best.

On two occasions, we took field trips to nearby attractions. We also walked, as a group, to the village ice cream parlor. After one week, it was hard to leave. I can't wait to repeat this experience, hopefully, many times in the future. I consider it a highlight and turning point in my life. It gives my life more meaning and will impact my future. I would never have expected to get to say that at 85 years of age?

After this week was over, I flew to my home in Phoenix, Arizona. A slightly interesting point is that when I had left on April 4th, I flew west to Hanoi, and when I returned, I flew from Warsaw, still flying west. It was the first time in my life to fly all the way around the world.

As I near the end of this memoir, I want to comment some more on my grieving process, which has been an underlying theme throughout. When I became aware that the process had happened to me in phases, I thought I had discovered something. I thought, "Perhaps this is profound enough to be of value to other people." From that moment on, as if by divine ordinance, every day, some book or article was brought to my attention regarding the 'phases of grief'. It really brought me down to earth. I have, because of this, had an insight that is perhaps worth sharing.

When you have a life-altering insight, it is good to share it. It may be helpful to someone, and some of these insights are worth recirculating regularly. But we should not, in our arrogance, think that they are new. If it is worthwhile, it is almost a sure thing that it has been observed and shared a million times before. Having said all that, I am still going to expound on my grief phases.

The first phase was extreme loneliness and loss - just life-consuming. I was not expecting that it would be physically painful. I tried to ignore it, but it was there all the time, all over me, like a heavy dark blanket.

The next phase was only a little lighter. It involved being able to talk about it when it was appropriate but, even more important, to stop talking about it all the time when it wasn't appropriate.

Shortly after this, I noticed that I could sometimes remember the things about my marriage to John that were not perfect. I really felt like this was a breakthrough. I sometimes thought, "You rascal! I should have made you stop that! If you were here now, things would be different!".

After this, I progressed to being so aware of the negatives that I proclaimed to myself, and some others, that if I could have John back, hale and healthy, I would not choose to do so. My life is pretty good now, and there are lots of positives to being alone. This phase lasted perhaps a year.

Then finally, I started remembering all the good times again. How much I enjoyed his company and how we shared the same interests, values, and sense of humor. How much we laughed at each other, how much we respected each other's intelligence! Oh, if I could only have him back, I most certainly would. But things would, indeed, be different. It is I who would change. All those negative things that I remember, I would gently remove them. It wouldn't require major surgery; it would require me to stop taking what the world gives me quietly. I would be more communicative; I would say what bothers me.

I know I have not learned it all, but there is quite a lot in this book about what I have learned. I hope it is helpful.

Summary: Life is not over until it is over. There is always more to do and enjoy. Most importantly, there is always someone to love. If you have love, cherish it. If you don't, look for it. When you are my age, love is not so limited as before. It comes in all ages, genders, and the most surprising places. When I think of all the oceans of people I have interacted with on this journey, I know that all of them, when my presence whispers across their memory, will smile and send me thanks for having been there. This generates a feeling of love and being loved that warms my heart more than I could ever describe.

When things go wrong, do not jump off the rig or take it quietly. Make an effort to fix it. If I had fixed the minor things, then I would not have had the small negatives to remember in phase three. That would have been better, but I don't spend time dwelling on it. That is over, and I can't change the past. All I have left is my memories and the future, and I am so blessed to have that.

Now I need to start planning my next trip, which I think will be to Dublin. Oh, and I must go see Vera. We missed our promised year—twice. But we are lucky to have both survived the horrible pandemic in good shape, so there is still time.

Warsaw library

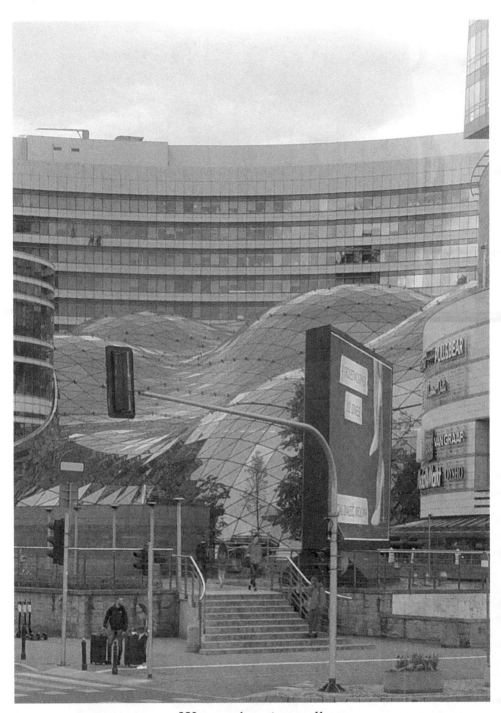

Warsaw shopping mall

Warsaw

Warsaw

Welcome home

The happy river

Zuzanna visits

Going to visit Vera

Wroclaw

Wroclaw

Angloville. Crazy fun and games

Angloville. Crazy fun and games

Angloville. Crazy fun and games

Angloville. Crazy fun and games

Angloville.

Made in the USA
Las Vegas, NV
14 March 2022

45632024R00184